Understanding AND **Using** THE **NAGLIERI** GENERAL ABILITY TESTS

Understanding AND Using THE NAGLIERI GENERAL ABILITY TESTS

A Call for EQUITY in Gifted Education

Dina M. Brulles, Ph.D.

Kimberly Lansdowne, Ph.D.

Jack A. Naglieri, Ph.D.

free spirit
PUBLISHING®

Library of Congress Cataloging-in-Publication Data
Names: Brulles, Dina, author. | Lansdowne, Kimberly, author. | Naglieri, Jack A., author.
Title: Understanding and using the Naglieri general ability tests : a call for equity in gifted education / Dina M. Brulles, PhD., Kimberly Lansdowne, Ph.D., Jack A. Naglieri, PhD.
Description: Huntington Beach : Free Spirit Publishing, an imprint of Teacher Created Materials, Inc., [2022] | Includes index.
Identifiers: LCCN 2022020576 (print) | LCCN 2022020577 (ebook) | ISBN 9781631986925 (paperback) ISBN 9781631986949 (ebook)
Subjects: LCSH: Gifted children—Education. | Educational tests and measurements. Educational equalization. | BISAC: EDUCATION / Special Education / Gifted | EDUCATION / Professional Development
Classification: LCC LC3993 .B694 2022 (print) | LCC LC3993 (ebook) | DDC 371.2601/3—dc23/ eng/20220609
LC record available at https://lccn.loc.gov/2022020576
LC ebook record available at https://lccn.loc.gov/2022020577

Edited by Cassandra Sitzman
Cover design by Shannon Pourciau; interior design by Grace Alba Le

Printed in the United States of America

Free Spirit Publishing
An imprint of Teacher Created Materials
6325 Sandburg Road, Suite 100
Minneapolis, MN 55427-3674
(612) 338-2068
help4kids@freespirit.com
freespirit.com

FSC
www.fsc.org
MIX
Paper from
responsible sources
FSC® C005010

Free Spirit offers competitive pricing.
Contact edsales@freespirit.com for pricing information on multiple quantity purchases.

Acknowledgments

Thank you to Free Spirit Publishing founder Judy Galbraith for recognizing the importance of educating teachers about gifted children and their unique social, emotional, and academic needs.

To Cassie Sitzman for her insightful and expert editing of this book.

To Multi-Health Systems for supporting and promoting our efforts to build equity and increase inclusion in gifted programs.

And to Rebekah West Keur for her insights and contributions to part three.

Contents

List of Figures

List of Reproducible Forms

To download the reproducible forms, visit freespirit.com/Naglieri.

Introduction

A Call for Equity in Gifted Education

In schools today, it is common to hear well-intentioned educators advocating for inclusion and equity, and many in society are calling for social justice and respect for diversity. Historical social injustices, along with common and often inequitable practices in education, have contributed to disparities in outcomes for generations of Black, Hispanic, and Native American students; English language learners; and students living in poverty. The Black Lives Matter movement has inspired many in the field of gifted education to reflect deeply on long-held and fundamentally flawed procedures, consider new approaches, and work to correct longstanding inequities surrounding gifted identification and programming.

In a statement published in the summer of 2020 by the National Association for Gifted Children (NAGC) titled "Championing Equity and Supporting Social Justice for Black Students in Gifted Education: An Expanded Vision for NAGC," they write: "In order to move forward, we must be prepared for challenging conversations about our past . . . as a field." They "acknowledge the injustices of structural and systemic racism and recognize the field of gifted education has historically been part of the problem by promoting these injustices, even if inadvertently."

This book strives to advance efforts to ensure that school policies provide access for *all* students who require the challenge of gifted education.

This book strongly adheres to this mindset and strives to advance efforts to ensure that school policies provide access for *all* students who require the challenge of gifted education. In the chapters that follow, we discuss failures in the field that perpetuate past inequities and offer new approaches for recognizing the high ability and potential of Black, Hispanic, and Native American students; English language learners; and students living in poverty so that they can be included in gifted education.

DEI in Gifted Identification and Programming

Diversity, equity, and inclusion (DEI) are paramount in education. So to begin the discussion, we ask that readers reflect on their interpretation and understanding of these terms in the context of the gifted services used and promoted in their schools. To understand how these constructs relate to gifted education, first consider some general information on these terms as commonly used in education systems.

Diversity refers to the psychological, physical, and social differences that occur among people, including but not limited to race, ethnicity, socioeconomic status, education, language, age, gender, and learning style. Diversity also refers to the presence of these differences within a given setting or group.

Equity guarantees fair treatment, access, opportunity, and advancement for all people. It acknowledges that historically underserved and underrepresented populations face unfair and unbalanced conditions that must be addressed to ensure their full participation. Equity recognizes that advantages and barriers exist and seeks to identify and correct these imbalances.

Inclusion is the act of creating environments in which any individual or group can be and feel welcomed, respected, supported, and valued to fully participate and bring their authentic selves. An inclusive and welcoming climate embraces differences and offers respect for the experiences, words, actions, and thoughts of all people.

In this book, we present ways to identify and serve all gifted students and build inclusive and diverse gifted programs. We rely on the diversity, equity, and inclusion constructs to frame our efforts and serve as guidelines for achieving these important goals. The descriptions and conversation that follow help educators consider these constructs within their schools' and districts' practices and procedures for gifted identification and services, specifically.

> **Diversity** requires proportional representation in a school's gifted services, which include identification procedures and programming options.

> **Equity** evaluates and finds the best ways to ensure accurate representation and create processes for identifying and serving historically underserved populations.

> **Inclusion** provides specific and meaningful practices that invite and honor diversity to create a welcoming and valued participation in gifted services.

Our Overarching Premise

This book is about identifying and serving gifted students, especially very smart students who have not been given the opportunity to participate in educational experiences that allow them to flourish academically and emotionally. We use the term *gifted* to designate a student who has high general ability, regardless of how much academic achievement they may have. Such students have tremendous potential to achieve academically and succeed in life, given opportunities to learn and develop their talents. A student can be gifted and not yet highly knowledgeable, which presents a dilemma that many schools wrestle with when creating gifted services.

We assert that the typical tests used to identify gifted students put excessive emphasis on content knowledge and English language proficiency. That is, the most widely used ability tests' academic content and verbal instructions pose an obstacle to equity in gifted identification, and they hamper efforts to achieve diversity in gifted programs. In addition, the way test data is used to determine admittance into gifted education programs further impacts the extent to which diversity and equity are achieved. For example, a requirement that students demonstrate high scores on tests that have verbal and quantitative content, even if they have a very high score on a nonverbal test, can block students with limited background knowledge and developing English language skills.

To address these obstacles, we describe an innovative trio of tests entitled the Naglieri General Ability Tests-Verbal (Naglieri and Brulles 2022), -Nonverbal (Naglieri 2022), and -Quantitative (Naglieri and Lansdowne 2022) that measure general ability using verbal, nonverbal, and quantitative content. These tests were developed specifically for identifying gifted students with little reliance on academic knowledge and English language skills, and they offer a more equitable approach to identifying and serving historically underrepresented students in gifted education.

Pertinent to this book is a critical analysis and understanding of the purpose of testing and how we can work toward the goal of increasing diversity and ensuring equity in gifted programs. Specifically, we question whether existing methods of testing for gifted identification appropriately serve our schools and students. If not, why then do we continue with the same procedures? We examine how test content can serve as an obstacle to equity in gifted identification and service, and we introduce an innovative method for identifying giftedness more equitably using the Naglieri General Ability Tests.

> The most widely used ability tests' academic content and verbal instructions pose an obstacle to equity in gifted identification, and they hamper efforts to achieve diversity in gifted programs.

Beyond considerations for identification and testing, we offer information intended to dispel a number of myths, but predominantly the myth that students with high ability who are not highly achieving cannot be gifted. We demonstrate how current methods for identifying and serving gifted students prevent some educators from recognizing high potential in students who have not yet attained high levels of academic achievement. Specifically, this refers to students who may not speak English fluently, students of color, culturally diverse learners, those who live in poverty or have lacked opportunities to learn prior to entering or while in school, and those with parents or guardians who are unfamiliar or uncomfortable with navigating the educational system.

About This Book

This book is written for all who are involved in gifted education, including teachers, administrators, and university faculty. For many years, we have known that there are disproportionate numbers of Black, Hispanic, and Native American students; English language learners; and students living in poverty in gifted education programs. *Understanding and Using the Naglieri General Ability Tests: A Call for Equity in Gifted Education* addresses these issues and provides strategies and suggestions to identify and enfranchise students who have previously been denied access.

This book is divided into three parts, all focused on identifying and providing services to the "invisible gifted," students who are really smart but have been left out of gifted services due to obtaining scores "below the cut."

Part One: Measuring General Ability

Part one sets the stage for the identification methods we suggest throughout the book. We begin by helping the reader understand how to interpret gifted test data to make decisions that increase diversity in the population of identified students.

Chapter 1 defines how test content serves as an obstacle to diversity in gifted identification and programs. In this chapter, we introduce a method for identifying giftedness more equitably through the use of the Naglieri General Ability Tests. We maintain that a test of ability (i.e., general intelligence) used to help identify gifted students should measure how well a student can think through problems to arrive at the correct answer rather than what they have learned. The Naglieri General Ability Tests are carefully designed to measure students' general ability: how well they can see relationships between ideas, words, numbers, and symbols; understand how various pieces fit the whole; recall verbal information; follow the sequences of things; and notice important distinctions between ideas or items.

Chapter 2 focuses on the impact traditional ability tests have had on underrepresentation of diverse students in gifted programs and what can be done to improve this. The solution hinges on a clear understanding of the way test instructions are presented, the nature of the test questions themselves, and the amount of background knowledge students need to answer the questions. We suggest that the goal of an ability test should be to measure how clearly a student can think to solve a problem, not what a student may or may not already know. This chapter provides research evidence showing that the verbal, nonverbal, and quantitative approach to measuring general ability can be made more equitable.

Part Two: Administering and Interpreting Ability Tests

In part two, we discuss test administration and how schools can use the results to identify and serve gifted student populations that are representative of the schools' demographics.

Chapter 3 offers suggestions for those administering the Naglieri General Ability Tests and provides recommendations for how schools can use test results. The chapter also defines logistical issues and practical procedures associated with gifted testing, and suggestions for successful implementation of testing in school and at home are explained.

The question of what happens after testing is completed is outlined in **chapter 4**. We describe a variety of ways to interpret and use test scores. We also illustrate methods for using local and national norms and provide suggestions for implementation.

Part Three: Instructional Approaches

Part three delves into culturally responsive teaching and proactive gifted programming that promotes equity and diversity.

Chapters 5 and 6 answer this question: *Once we identify diverse students, how do we include them in our gifted programs?* Once a gifted student is identified based on their ability to think clearly and deeply, then educators must work to provide curricula that meet the student's academic needs. In essence, this means that school administrators need to establish a system wherein the curriculum and instruction develop and support the advanced learning needs of students of all racial, ethnic, linguistic, and economic backgrounds.

How to Use This Book

Although this book is divided into three parts, we recommend that educators first read it in its entirety. Once read, the parts can be utilized by different groups within a school or school district for different purposes.

Ideally, part one should be read by all people involved in gifted education since it addresses the social justice issues prevalent in identifying gifted students. These two chapters can be used in a class on testing and measurement, as a book study, or in a professional development seminar for teachers.

Part two is all about ability tests: how to administer them and what to do once the testing is complete. These chapters are more focused on teacher understanding and development, but should also be read by school-level administrators. Some ideas for how to use the chapters in part two include as part of whole-school staff development, in a study for a professional learning community, and, most importantly, with gifted education coordinators and gifted education teachers.

Part three describes what happens once students are identified. These chapters will help general education classroom teachers, gifted classroom teachers, and special education teachers understand the learning needs of underrepresented populations. They should be mandatory readings for all teachers who work with gifted students.

We wrote this book to share new and innovative methods for increasing equity and diversity in gifted programs. We hope that the procedures and practices described here provide educators with impetus to make changes that result in more inclusive gifted programs and services. By replacing barriers with the promising practices described herein, educators and schools can begin to address social injustice in gifted education.

> We wrote this book to share new and innovative methods for increasing equity and diversity in gifted programs. By replacing barriers with the promising practices described herein, educators and schools can begin to address social injustice in gifted education.

PART 1
Measuring General Ability

The Elephant in the Room

Underrepresentation of Black, Hispanic, and Native American students; English language learners; and students living in poverty has for decades been the elephant in the room in gifted education. We are now in a reawakening about this problem of undereducating more than a million students in grades K–12 today. In this chapter, we describe the depth of the problem. We also describe how to address it and the research supporting our solutions. We explain how the most widely available ability tests have contributed to underrepresentation and exactly what can be done to remedy their weaknesses.

Room for Improvement

It's often said that the biggest room in the world is the room for improvement. The research and data shared here clearly demonstrate that, despite efforts from scholars, researchers, and practitioners in the field of gifted education, educators continue to wrestle with finding solutions to address the underrepresentation of Black, Hispanic, and Native American students; English language learners; and students living in poverty. We can—and must—do better.

It is clear that the procedures used to identify gifted students play a key role in the extent to which the population of the gifted program reflects the composition of a school and school district. And they pose a major obstacle to achieving equitable representation. It is a complex issue, and administrators responsible for identifying gifted students face many challenges, such as how to:

➤ decide which tests to use

➤ include qualitative information

➤ reconcile school grades with ability test scores

➤ choose between ability tests that provide verbal, nonverbal, and quantitative scores versus tests that only provide a nonverbal score

➤ ensure that the curriculum meets the needs of the students

➤ combine multiple sources of information as dictated by state mandates

➤ manage the pressures from stakeholders, including school administrators, teachers, and parents

Despite these challenges, the field of gifted education must reevaluate identification processes and do more to ensure that historically underrepresented students have an equal opportunity to achieve. Perhaps some of the most influential factors contributing to underrepresentation are the ability tests used to identify gifted students. As Ford (2013) and Naglieri and Ford (2003) suggested, ability tests that contain verbal and quantitative knowledge have limited the representation of students of color, English language learners, and students living in poverty in gifted programs.

So, what do we know about the extent to which students of color are underrepresented? The *Digest of Education Statistics* report from the National Center for Education Statistics (NCES) provides demographic information about students in US public schools in general, and those in programs for the gifted and talented in particular. For example, enrollments in public elementary and secondary schools (table 203.60 of the *Digest*) provide important demographic information that can be used to better understand the degree to which students in gifted programs accurately represent the population of students in the United States. The total number of public school students entering preK through grade 12 for 2014 was estimated to be 50.30 million. The number of students by race and ethnicity that could have been identified as gifted can be calculated using the number of students identified as gifted (from table 204.80 of the *Digest*) and the number of potentially gifted students by race and ethnicity.

> Educators continue to wrestle with finding solutions to address the underrepresentation of Black, Hispanic, and Native American students; English language learners; and students living in poverty. We can—and must—do better.

Although it is often thought that gifted students represent the top 10 percent of a population, we used a more conservative 8 percent (92nd percentile) to compute the number of students who were and were not identified. The results (see **figure 1.1**) show that approximately 290,000 Black and 547,000 Hispanic students could have been identified as gifted and were not. Native Americans and those with two or more races were also underrepresented by 11,000 and 26,000 students, respectively. These results illustrate the inequities present in gifted programs; White students were identified at a rate similar to the percentage enrolled in the public schools, but that was not true for students of color. Black and Hispanic students were underidentified by a little more than 50 percent, Native American students by approximately 70 percent, and those having two or more races by 80 percent. The total number of non-White students who were missed in gifted identification was approximately 873,000.

FIGURE 1.1 Number of Students Enrolled in US Public Schools in 2018: Total Enrollment and Gifted Enrollment by Race and Ethnicity

	Students enrolled in K–12 public schools	Potentially gifted students (8 percent; 92nd percentile)	Students identified for gifted programs	Difference between potentially gifted and identified students	Representation ratio
White	23,834,458	1,906,757	1,937,350	30,593	102%
Black	7,754,506	620,360	330,774	-289,586	53%
Hispanic	14,337,467	1,146,997	600,498	-546,499	52%
Native American/ Alaska Native	484,766	38,781	27,712	-11,069	71%
Two or More Races	1,641,817	131,345	105,371	-25,974	80%
Total Non-White Students	24,218,556	1,937,484	1,064,355	-873,129	55%

Notes:
1. Representation ratio was calculated as follows: Students identified for gifted programs / Potentially gifted students.
2. K–12 enrollment data is from table 203.60 of the *Digest for Education Statistics*: "Enrollment and Percentage Distribution of Enrollment in Public Elementary and Secondary Schools, by Race/Ethnicity and Level of Education: Fall 1999 Through Fall 2027." nces.ed.gov/programs/digest/d17/tables/dt17_203.60.asp.
3. Gifted enrollment data is from table 204.80 of the *Digest for Education Statistics*: "Number of Public-School Students Enrolled in Gifted and Talented Programs, by Sex, Race/Ethnicity, and State: Selected Years, 2004 Through 2013–14." nces.ed.gov/programs/digest/d17/tables/dt17_204.80.asp.

It is important to note that the estimate presented in figure 1.1 represents the 873,129 students who were tested and not identified in the states that have procedures for finding gifted students. According to Gentry et al. (2019), 41.5 percent of schools in the United States do not assess students for gifted programs. If we add 41.5 percent to the value of 873,129, the total estimated number of students of color missed due to unfair methods of assessment or no assessment at all is 1,235,434.

Underrepresentation of students who are English language learners is also a problem, as shown in the Office for Civil Rights *2013–2014 Civil Rights Data Collection* report. The data revealed that even though they made up 11 percent of all students in schools offering gifted programs, they represented fewer than 3 percent of students actually in those gifted programs. Using the same procedures as in figure 1.1, **figure 1.2** shows that about 250,000 students learning English could have been identified for gifted programs but were not. Of that group, most were Hispanic students. Using the same adjustment to the numbers of students learning English that was made for students of color, the number of unidentified gifted English language learners increases to 329,018.

Equitable representation of students of color, English language learners, and students living in poverty in gifted education is not just an important issue for gifted educators; it is a critical social justice issue that has considerable implications for the entire field of education, the course of many students' lives, and the country as a whole. When such large numbers of students in US public education are missed in gifted identification, a significant portion of the school population goes undereducated. Educators in the United States should not exclude these smart students, especially because for the first time, non-White students represent more than half of the current public school population (Domenech, Sherman, and Brown 2016). We are encouraged by the increasing recognition in the field of education that this should and can be addressed. And the first steps are to use better tests to identify gifted students, consider local norms in addition to national norms when testing, and ensure that the manner in which eligibility decisions are made is focused on equity.

> Equitable representation of students of color, English language learners, and students living in poverty in gifted education is a critical social justice issue that has considerable implications for the entire field of education, the course of many students' lives, and the country as a whole.

FIGURE 1.2 Number of English Language Learner (ELL) Students Enrolled in US Public Schools: Total Enrollment and Gifted Enrollment by Race and Ethnicity

	ELL students enrolled in K–12 public schools	Potentially gifted ELL students (8 percent; 92nd percentile)	ELL students identified for gifted programs	Difference between potentially gifted and identified students	Representation ratio
White	294,763	23,581	8,548	-15,033	36.2%
Black	178,141	14,251	5,166	-9,085	36.2%

Hispanic	3,772,633	301,811	109,406	-192,405	36.2%
Asian	511,703	40,936	14,839	-26,097	36.2%
Pacific Islander	26,992	2,159	783	-1,376	36.3%
Native American/ Alaska Native	38,792	3,103	1,125	-1,978	36.3%
Two or More Races	31,136	2,491	903	-1,588	36.3%
Total Non-White Students	4,559,397	364,752	132,222	-232,530	36.2%

Notes:

1. Representation ratio was calculated as follows: ELL students identified for gifted programs / Potentially gifted ELL students.
2. The number of students identified was based on Office for Civil Rights *2013–2014 Civil Rights Data Collection* report, revised in 2016. ed.gov/about/offices/list/ocr/docs/2013-14-first-look.pdf.

Test Content Matters

To ensure that all students have an equal opportunity to do as well as they can on a measure of ability, test questions should measure how well students can *think*, and scores should not be influenced by how much they *know*. This is important for fair and equitable evaluation. It is well documented that the amount of knowledge (general information, verbal facts, and math facts) students attain is related to the amount of enrichment they receive. So, if a student has, for example, limited opportunity to learn the English language, and if a measure of intelligence given to the student includes tests of vocabulary or arithmetic word problems, then the student's score on the measure of intelligence will be influenced by the knowledge the student has or has not yet acquired.

This is a fundamental limitation of traditional intelligence tests that is addressed in the *Standards for Educational and Psychological Testing* (AERA, APA, NCME 2014). The authors assert that even if an IQ test does not show evidence of bias, based on a number of psychometric criteria, that test could still be unfair. The *Standards* state that if a person has had limited opportunities to learn the content in a test of intelligence, that test may be considered unfair because it penalizes students for not knowing the answers even if there is no evidence of psychometric test bias. Thus, equitable assessment means that all examinees have an equal opportunity to display their ability.

Differentiating between test bias (psychometric analyses such as factor analysis and item difficulty gradients) and equity (the impact a test's content has on the scores and the students evaluated) has very practical implications: it determines who is identified as gifted, and who is not.

There is another, less obvious, implication as well: test equity is about *how* general ability is measured. There is a long history of using verbal and quantitative test questions to measure general intelligence, and this practice persists to this day. It can be illustrated by Lynn's (2010, 95) assertion, "Scores on [reading comprehension and mathematics can be] used as a proxy for IQs, . . . [because a] reading test is a measure of verbal comprehension and [a] mathematics test is a measure of 'quantitative reasoning,' and both of these are major components of general intelligence (e.g., Carroll 1993, 597; McGrew and Flanagan 1998, 14–15)." This belief is shared by some theoreticians, but not others (e.g., Naglieri and Otero 2017). In our view, tests relying on questions that measure knowledge confound the measurement of general intelligence.

Even so, examples of these kinds of questions on tests of intelligence are plentiful. In the current version of the Woodcock-Johnson IV *achievement* test is a reading vocabulary-synonyms subtest that has the following prompt: "Tell me another word for *large*." Correct answers are *big, enormous, gigantic*, and *huge*. The Woodcock-Johnson IV *cognitive* ability test has an oral vocabulary subtest which has this prompt: "Tell me another word for *big*." Correct answers are *large, gigantic*, and *huge*. This is just one of many examples of the similarity between achievement and ability test items (see Naglieri 2008 for more) and the acceptance of this practice by researchers and practitioners.

A good example of the impact test content can have on the evaluation of children's general ability is provided by the study by Lynn (2010). Using reading and math scores from the 2007 PISA Study by the Organization for Economic Co-operation and Development as a measure of general ability, Lynn concluded, "The lower IQ in southern Italy may be attributable to genetic admixture with populations from the Near East and North Africa" (93). This conclusion ignores the *Standards for Educational and Psychological Testing* assertion that test content poses an equity problem, just as Yoakum and Yerkes (1920) and Pintner (1923) noted one hundred years ago. Importantly, Lynn's conclusions were refuted by D'Amico et al. (2012), who reported similar scores of southern and northern Italian children on Raven's Progressive Matrices and when using the PASS theory of intelligence as measured by the Italian version of the Cognitive Assessment System (Naglieri and Das 2006). D'Amico et al. argued that the differences in verbal and math scores reflected differences in children's educational opportunity, not their intelligence, and the researchers' results clearly supported this conclusion.

The connection between opportunity to learn and ability test scores was also shown in a study by Kaya, Stough, and Juntune (2016). They found that low-income students in the United States had significantly lower verbal than nonverbal scores on the Otis-Lennon School Ability Test (OLSAT), which they attributed to poverty's influence on the development of the students' verbal skills. Still, some defend the inclusion of verbal and quantitative test items that demand knowledge by arguing that "verbal and quantitative abilities . . . add importantly to the prediction of academic success" (Lohman, Korb, and Lakin 2008, 276). This argument ignores the similarity in test content across ability and achievement tests.

It is illogical to argue that test questions that require knowledge of language and math word problems on tests such as the CogAT and OLSAT have validity because they correlate with tests of reading and math skills on an achievement test. Like the Woodcock-Johnson IV example provided above, these tests use very similar questions on measures of ability and achievement—presumably different kinds of tests that *should* be asking different kinds of questions. Using questions that demand knowledge in a test of ability means that students with limited opportunity to acquire knowledge will obtain inaccurately lower scores. Our view is simple: a test of ability should measure how well a student can think to solve problems and should be minimally influenced by what the student knows.

> A test of ability should measure how well a student can think to solve problems and should be minimally influenced by what the student knows.

The advantage of using a nonverbal test that requires a minimal amount of knowledge was illustrated by Naglieri, Booth, and Winsler (2004). They found that Spanish-speaking Hispanic students in the United States with limited English language proficiency earned considerably lower scores on SAT-9 Reading and Verbal than a matched sample of Hispanic students who were proficient in English. These groups did *not* differ, however, on the Naglieri Nonverbal Ability Test (NNAT), because that test measures thinking in a way that is not confounded by knowledge.

We categorically reject the use of test questions so obviously dependent upon English-language fluency and academic skills taught in school as a means of measuring general ability because of the barriers to equity that this approach erects and the harmful impacts it has. Ultimately, how much of a problem this presents depends upon which ability tests are used.

Measuring Ability Using Achievement

The use of test questions on group- and individually administered ability tests (i.e., traditional intelligence tests) that are indistinguishable from those on tests of achievement is steeped in tradition. Nearly all ability tests include verbal (vocabulary, word analogies) and quantitative (math word problems) questions. These are often described as a measure of one's verbal or quantitative *reasoning ability* rather than one's *knowledge and skill* with words and math. It is critically important that the content of the questions found on tests of intelligence and tests of achievement be different (Naglieri and Otero 2017). Verbal, nonverbal, and quantitative items have been used on ability/intelligence tests since the early 1900s, and they form the basis of such tests as the Wechsler, the OLSAT, and the CogAT (Gibbons and Warne 2019). The foundations for these tests are also in the original work of Binet and in the *Army Mental Tests*, which were developed in the early 1900s to evaluate recruits for World War I (Yoakum and Yerkes 1920). In all of these examples, test questions that demanded knowledge were used to measure intelligence.

The authors of the *Army Mental Tests* recognized that certain parts of the Army Alpha (a verbal and quantitative test) posed a problem for the uneducated. In fact, they wrote, "Men who fail in Alpha [verbal and quantitative test questions] are sent to Beta [nonverbal test questions] in order that injustice by reason of relative unfamiliarity with English may be avoided" (Yoakum and Yerkes 1920, 19). Another test author of that time, Rudolf Pintner (1923), was more specific, writing that "a good intelligence test must avoid as much as possible anything that is commonly learned by the subjects tested. In a broad sense this rests on a differentiation between knowledge and intelligence" (61). Yet the practice continued.

Many years later, in the very influential 1972 book *Wechsler's Measurement and Appraisal of Adult Intelligence,* Matarazzo noted the obvious connection between educational opportunity and scores on the vocabulary and arithmetic subtests. He stated, "A man's vocabulary is necessarily influenced by his education and cultural opportunities" (218). Referring to the arithmetic subtest, he said, "Its merits are lessened by the fact that it is influenced by education" (203). Two and a half decades later, in 1997, Suzuki and Valencia stated that verbal and quantitative test items included in traditional intelligence tests interfere with accurate assessment of Black, Hispanic, and Native American students. This was illustrated by Naglieri and Yazzie (1983), who found that Navajo children living on a reservation in northern Arizona who had not experienced any learning problems had low scores on the verbal scales of the Wechsler but average scores on the nonverbal scales. They determined that this difference was due to English being the children's second language, so the children had less exposure to the language used by the students in the normative group.

It is critically important that the content of the questions found on tests of intelligence and tests of achievement be different.

The recognition of the confounding effect of knowledge in tests of intelligence has been known for decades, yet this fundamental limitation has been largely ignored by researchers, practitioners, and publishers of such tests. In fact, most individually administered ability tests used by psychologists today in educational and other settings, as well as the group-administered tests used to identify gifted students, contain questions that demand knowledge of words and math word problems. This is a fundamental flaw that confounds the measurement of ability with what a student knows and is one of the reasons why we suggest, as Yoakum and Yerkes did more than one hundred years ago, that the content of these tests poses a barrier to equity and thereby is a social justice issue.

Our concerns about the damaging impact traditional intelligence tests with academic content have had on the education of gifted students and more broadly on society were recognized in the American Psychological Association's 2021 "Apology to People of Color for APA's Role in Promoting, Perpetuating, and

Failing to Challenge Racism, Racial Discrimination, and Human Hierarchy in the U.S." This apology included the role psychologists played in "creat[ing] and promot[ing] the use of psychological tests and instruments that have been used to disadvantage many communities of color, contributing to the overdiagnosis, misdiagnosis, and lack of culturally appropriate diagnostic criteria." The apology highlights the "roles of psychology and [the] APA in promoting, perpetuating, and failing to challenge racism, and the harms that have been inflicted on communities of color," and notes the role intelligence tests have played to systemically "create the ideology of white supremacy and harm communities of color." This apology amplifies the importance of our efforts to create equitable measures of intelligence.

Chapter Summary

We maintain that a test of ability (or general intelligence) used to help identify gifted students should measure how well a student can think through problems to arrive at the correct answer. We further assert that tests of general ability with verbal, quantitative, and nonverbal content could be equitable if constructed differently than they have been. Such tests should be designed to measure how well students can see relationships between ideas, words, numbers, and symbols; understand how various pieces fit the whole; recall verbal information; follow the sequences of things; and notice important distinctions between ideas or things, all of which can be described as general ability (Naglieri, Brulles, and Lansdowne 2009). We propose that general ability can be assessed in an equitable manner if academic skills are omitted from the measurement of intelligence (Naglieri 1982; Naglieri, Brulles, and Lansdowne 2021).

CHAPTER

2
Ability Tests for Gifted Identification: Old and New Solutions

In this chapter, we focus on the impact traditional ability tests have had on who is identified for gifted programs and what can be done to improve the situation. The solution hinges on a clear understanding of the way a test's instructions are presented, the nature of the test questions themselves, and the amount of knowledge required of the student to answer the questions. This chapter provides research evidence showing that the verbal, nonverbal, and quantitative approach to measuring general ability can be made more equitable.

A Little History

Measuring general ability using verbal, nonverbal, and quantitative questions has been widely practiced since the early 1900s, when the *US Army Mental Tests* were developed to evaluate recruits for World War I (Yoakum and Yerkes 1920). The authors of the Army Alpha (verbal and quantitative) and Beta (nonverbal) developed tests that would be "adaptable for group use for the examining of large numbers rapidly . . . [and] have a high degree of validity as a measure of [general] intelligence" (Yoakum and Yerkes 1920, 2). These tests were assembled without the benefit of a theoretical definition of intelligence. As Pintner (1923) explained, "We did not start with a clear definition of general intelligence . . . [but] borrowed from everyday life a vague term implying all-round ability and knowledge . . . [and we are] still attempting to define it more sharply and endow it with a stricter scientific connotation" (53).

The Army Alpha and Beta tests (as well as the work of Binet and Simon) were the foundation of all traditional intelligence tests. The description of general intelligence provided by Pintner is similar to the one provided by Wechsler: "The aggregate or global capacity of the individual to act purposefully, to think rationally, and to deal effectively with his environment" (1939, 79). This too is a definition that could benefit from further explanation. In an attempt to clarify the term *general ability*, Naglieri, Brulles, and Lansdowne (2009) described it as what "allows people to solve a number of different kinds of problems that may involve words, pictures, sounds, or numbers, and that may require verbal, quantitative, or nonverbal reasoning, memory, sequencing, pattern recognition, insights, drawing inferences, and analyzing simple and complex ideas" (129).

It is important to recognize that there was no assumption that the Army Alpha or Beta measured different *kinds of abilities*, but rather *one general ability* initially represented by the single letter *g* by Charles Spearman in 1904. He was the first to describe the existence of general intelligence, which he proposed was responsible for overall performance on mental ability tests. Spearman had considerable influence on Wechsler.

Canivez, Watkins, and Dombrowski (2017) asserted that general ability, which is represented by the total score, has the most validity of all the scores traditional ability tests provide. That is, the idea that verbal and nonverbal test scores represent distinct abilities is *not* supported in research. This suggestion is consistent with statements by Yoakum, Yerkes, Pintner, and Wechsler, who did not suggest that different types of intelligences were being measured by verbal, quantitative, and nonverbal tests, but rather that using different ways to measure "general ability" had advantages.

Kaufman (2006) reminds us that "Wechsler remained a firm believer in Spearman's *g* theory throughout his lifetime. He believed that his Verbal and Performance Scales represented different ways to access *g*, but he never believed in nonverbal [or verbal] intelligence as being separate from *g*. Rather, he saw the Performance Scale [Wechsler's nonverbal scale] as the most sensible way to measure the general intelligence of people with hearing impairments, language disorders, or limited proficiency in English" (iv).

Measuring general ability using traditional verbal and quantitative tests that demand verbal comprehension of instructions and are laden with knowledge-based questions creates a dilemma because the scores reflect a student's ability to think (reason) *in a way that is confounded by* what they know. For example, a vocabulary test given in English can be considered an accurate way to measure a student's knowledge of words if that student knows English. When a vocabulary or word analogy test is used in a test of *general ability*, however, the scores are not so accurate. They reflect what a student has learned—that is, the student's proficiency with the English language—along with their ability to arrive at the answer by thinking. Thus, the measurement of ability becomes confounded by what the student knows.

Thinking and Knowing Continuum

Not all tests of general ability require knowledge to the same degree. For example, some tests are similar to the Army Alpha and Beta in that they have verbal, nonverbal, and quantitative content (e.g., OLSAT, CogAT, WISC-V). Some have only questions that demand knowledge of words (e.g., Peabody Picture Vocabulary Test), and others use diagrams and are typically called nonverbal tests (e.g., Naglieri Nonverbal Ability Test, Wechsler Nonverbal Scale of Ability). Ability tests can be placed on a continuum based on the amount of knowledge required in the test questions and the directions used during administration. For example, on one end of the continuum are tests such as the Stanford Achievement Test or the Iowa Test of Basic Skills that are designed to measure what students have learned from the curriculum they have been exposed to. At the other end of the continuum are tests such as the Naglieri Nonverbal Ability Test, which demand very little acquired knowledge and instead require thinking to recognize the logic in the way shapes and colors are organized and change across a progressive matrix.

We estimated the amount of knowledge included in the most widely used tests and the frequency those tests were used for identification of gifted students according to Kurtz et al. (2019). The number of scales in each test that require knowledge was determined and expressed as a percentage of the total number of scales. **Figures 2.1** and **2.2** provide our estimates of the amount of knowledge included in the tests and the frequency of test use. We included the Iowa Test of Basic Skills (an achievement test) because it is commonly used for gifted identification even though, by definition, it is a test completely designed to measure knowledge and skills.

FIGURE 2.1. Amount of Knowledge Included in Common Ability Tests

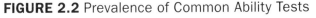

FIGURE 2.2 Prevalence of Common Ability Tests

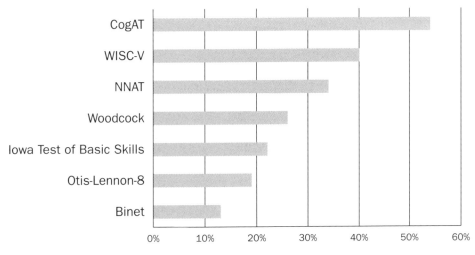

The information provided in the figures shows that of the three ability tests most commonly used to identify gifted students, two require a considerable amount of knowledge (CogAT, 66 percent and WISC-V, 40 percent) and one essentially requires no acquired knowledge (NNAT, 5 percent). It is important to recognize that these estimates provide only a partial picture. They do not include the amount of knowledge required for students to understand the directions for taking the tests, which can be substantial, nor do they reflect whether the tests require students to verbally provide answers.

Equity, Test Scores, and Identifying Gifted Students

Chapter 1 explained that the *Standards for Educational and Psychological Testing* measure test equity by the impact that questions that require knowledge have on the results of a test. It is important to ask if there is evidence that tests that require knowledge yield different average scores across racial and ethnic demographics and therefore influence who is identified. This question has been explored for both group- and individually administered tests used to identify gifted students. **Figure 2.3** provides a summary of the available research.

FIGURE 2.3 Intelligence Test Mean Standard Score Differences by Race and Ethnicity

	Average Score Difference by Race	Average Score Difference by Ethnicity
Tests that require knowledge	Mn = 11.5	Mn = 9.2
Otis-Lennon School Ability Test	13.6	
Stanford-Binet IV (normative sample)	12.6	
WISC-V (normative sample)	11.6	
WJ- III (normative sample)	10.9	10.7
CogAT7 (nonverbal scale)	11.8	7.6
WISC-V (statistical controls normative sample)	8.7	
Tests that require minimal knowledge	Mn = 4.1	Mn = 2.6
K-ABC (normative sample)	7.0	
K-ABC (matched sample)	6.1	
CAS2 (normative sample)	6.3	4.5

	Average Score Difference by Race	Average Score Difference by Ethnicity
CAS (statistical controls normative sample)	4.8	4.8
CAS2 (statistical controls normative sample)	4.3	1.8
CAS2 Brief (statistical controls normative samples)	2.0	2.8
NNAT (matched samples)	4.2	2.8
Naglieri General Ability Test-Verbal	2.2	1.6
Naglieri General Ability Test-Nonverbal	1.0	1.1
Naglieri General Ability Test-Quantitative	3.2	1.3

Note: The results summarized here were reported for the Otis-Lennon School Ability Test by Avant and O'Neal (1986); Stanford-Binet IV by Wasserman and Becker (2000); Woodcock-Johnson III race differences by Edwards and Oakland (2006) and ethnic differences by Sotelo-Dynega, Ortiz, Flanagan, and Chaplin (2013); CogAT7 by Carman, Walther, and Bartsch (2018); WISC-V by Kaufman, Raiford, and Coalson (2016); Kaufman Assessment Battery for Children-II by Lichtenberger, Sotelo-Dynega, and Kaufman (2009) and Naglieri (1986); CAS by Naglieri, Rojahn, Matto, and Aquilino (2005); CAS2 and CAS2 Brief by Naglieri, Das, and Goldstein (2014a, 2014b); Naglieri Nonverbal Ability Test by Naglieri and Ronning (2000), and Naglieri General Ability Tests by Naglieri, Brulles, and Lansdowne (2021).

. . . .

These results are very informative. Viewed as a whole, they show that tests requiring knowledge yield large average score differences in full-scale standard scores by race and ethnicity. Tests that demand knowledge are more difficult for students who have less background knowledge and/or emerging English-language skills, and the result is lower scores. In contrast, those group-administered tests (NNAT and Naglieri General Ability Tests) and individually administered tests (Cognitive Assessment System, or CAS and CAS2) that require minimal knowledge yield considerably smaller average score differences by race and ethnicity.

Large differences in average test scores are important evidence related to equity, but so too are the numbers of students by race and ethnicity who earn scores high enough to be considered gifted. Naglieri and Ford (2003) examined the effectiveness of the NNAT in identifying gifted Black, Hispanic, and White students. The sample consisted of 20,270 students in grades K–12 that was representative of the US population on several demographic variables. They found similar percentages of White (5.6 percent), Black (5.1 percent), and Hispanic (4.4 percent) students earned a standard score of 125 (95th percentile rank), supporting the use of this nonverbal test for the equitable identification of students for gifted education services.

Another excellent large-scale study of identification rates involved approximately 3,000 students and was conducted by Durtschi (2019). She examined the relationships between race and identification rates using the 90th and 95th percentile scores from the Cognitive Abilities Test 7 (CogAT7). Durtschi found a significant difference between racial groups in CogAT7 scores, which resulted in the underrepresentation of Black and Hispanic students. Finally, Carman, Walther, and Bartsch (2018) also found significant differences between the CogAT7 nonverbal scores by race and ethnicity. They reported that Black and Hispanic students earned scores that were 11.8 and 7.6 standard score points less than White students' scores, respectively.

Tests that require knowledge yield large differences across race and ethnicity, which negatively impact test scores and the numbers of students of color who qualify for gifted educational services.

Naglieri and Ford (2005) provide another example of how test items can pose a problem for students with limited English reading skills. They evaluated the reading levels required for the sentence completion test on the CogAT Form 6, Level D, which is taken by children in grades 5 and 6. Using the Flesch-Kincaid Grade Level method, they determined the readability of the test items was a grade level score of 6.1, with readabilities of the individual items ranging from grade 3.7 to grade 10.4. Children with poor English reading skills, therefore, are likely to earn low scores on this kind of test because of its reading-level demands.

In summary, these research studies show a clear pattern related to the amount of knowledge required by a test and its equity. Those tests that require knowledge yield large differences across race and ethnicity, which negatively impact test scores and the numbers of students of color who qualify for gifted educational services. The large differences in scores by race and ethnicity on the CogAT7 nonverbal battery are likely due to lengthy oral directions that demand considerable verbal comprehension. The CogAT7 results are inconsistent with the results shown for the NNAT and the Naglieri General Ability Tests-Nonverbal, which use pictorial and animated instructions, respectively.

Test Directions and Responses Required

The assessment process places many demands upon the student being examined beyond answering the questions included in a test of intelligence. Some tests, for example, require that a student can verbally articulate answers to questions and their response is scored based on the level of sophistication. Verbal expression becomes a contributor to the final obtained score. Another factor is comprehension of verbal instructions. A student may not understand directions that contain verbal concepts, or the student may not have had much experience learning the language the examiner is using. These two aspects of testing are important for equitable assessment of intelligence.

Verbal Directions

The directions for ability tests should be carefully prepared to ensure students understand what to do. To standardize test administration, teachers or other professionals who proctor exams are given a script to read to provide detailed instructions to students. Just like test content, test directions can pose a barrier to equity. Directions might require knowledge that students do not have. This was shown by Cummings and Nelson (1980), who analyzed oral directions for the presence of Boehm's basic concepts in several group-administered achievement tests. They found, for example, that the instructions for the California Achievement Test and the Iowa Test of Basic Skills included many basic concepts that students may not have mastered at the ages for which the tests were intended. More recently, Gill et al. (2012) noted that difficulty following directions can be related to underlying problems with grammar and semantic aspects of language such as listening comprehension. Engle, Carullo, and Collins (1991) found that students' ability to recall directions presented orally in the classroom was related to their working memory capacity.

To illustrate this issue, consider the directions in one of the tasks on the most widely used group-administered test's nonverbal scale. The directions, intended for administration to five- and six-year-olds, contain about thirty lines of text and approximately four hundred words. Furthermore, many verbal concepts are included in the directions, and some of the statements are complex. For example: "The small circle goes with the large circle in the same way that the small square goes with the large square." In this item, the inclusion of verbal concepts (small, large, circle, square), the grammatical structure, and the strain on working memory can impact students' reading and listening comprehension. They can also be an obstacle to understanding the demands of the task for students with limited verbal skills.

Verbal Expression

A similar barrier to equity exists when students must communicate an answer by speaking to the examiner. Traditional individually administered ability tests require students to explain, for example, in what way an apple and a pear are the same or the meaning of vocabulary words. The quality of the response is graded 0, 1, or 2 based on rules established by the test authors. This method of assessment gives advantage to students with a well-developed vocabulary and verbal expression skills, but it disadvantages those with limited verbal knowledge and skills.

A Simple Solution

Three threats to the accuracy and validity of traditional group- and individually administered ability tests used to identify gifted students are test content, test directions, and the need for a verbal response from the student. All three of these threats, however, can be managed by the way tests are constructed. For example, when we constructed the Naglieri General Ability Tests, our overarching goal was to create an equitable test of general ability that measured thinking across three content areas in a way that was minimally related to formal educational opportunities.

To achieve this goal, the verbal, quantitative, and nonverbal scales include questions that can be solved using any language. The directions for administration are presented using a video demonstration (online version) or pictorial depictions (paper version). The tests do not require students to verbally explain their answers. We now have excellent research (see the section "Evidence for the Naglieri General Ability Tests" on page 28) that shows this approach is a highly effective way to measure general ability. It also provides an equitable method for assessing ability of diverse populations in general, and specifically as part of the identification of gifted students.

Description of the Naglieri General Ability Tests: Verbal, Nonverbal, and Quantitative

The Naglieri General Ability Tests use verbal, nonverbal, and quantitative test questions. These three separate tests were developed to measure general intellectual ability in as fair a manner as possible when administered individually or to groups using online or paper formats. Each of the tests takes approximately thirty minutes and is intended for students in grades K–9. And each has three key elements:

➤ Test items consist of questions presented using diagrams, numbers, and pictures so that minimal academic knowledge is needed.

➤ Test questions can be solved regardless of the language(s) spoken by the student.

➤ No oral responses are required.

Test Content

Although the three tests were constructed using questions that have verbal, nonverbal, or quantitative content, they all measure general ability.

The verbal test measures general ability using questions that require a student to recognize a verbal concept when that concept is represented in pictures. The student must closely evaluate and understand what each picture is, what characteristics it has, and what trait or relationship unites five of the six pictures to identify which one does not represent the concept. The nonverbal test uses questions that require a student to carefully examine the relationships among shapes presented in a pattern, using sequences, spatial orientations, and other distinguishing characteristics to arrive at the correct answer. The quantitative test measures general ability using questions that require a student to closely examine the relationships among numbers and/or symbols, numerical sequences, equivalency, and patterns involving basic math to determine the correct answer.

Test Instructions and Responses

Instructions to the students are presented using animated videos when taken online or a four-frame pictorial version of the video when administered on paper. This method eliminates the need for comprehension of verbal instructions because students are *shown* what they need to do. This approach also eliminates a demand on working memory since students can play or view the instructions as many times as needed. To eliminate the role of verbal expression in the tests, students respond using a multiple-choice format.

These methods were used so that general ability could be measured using tests that vary in content and can be solved using any language.

Verbal Test

The Naglieri General Ability Tests-Verbal (Naglieri-V) measures general ability using pictures of ordinary objects that represent a verbal concept. The test questions contain universally recognized pictures that do not rely on information typically obtained in school and that are common across cultures. Students are required to identify which five of the six pictures shown represent a verbal concept that is not shared by the sixth picture.

The Naglieri-V test items, like those in the quantitative and nonverbal tests, are solved by careful consideration of the relationships among the pictures provided. The questions require close examination of the attributes of the images (color, use, function, orientation, etc.), reflection of those attributes across images, consideration of possible connections among the images, and reasoning to find how five of the six go together. The use of pictures to represent verbal concepts rather than written or spoken words allows the student to solve the task regardless of the language(s) used. For example, if the verbal concept of fruit were presented in written form, it might look something like this: Apple, Orange, Pear, Bowl, Grape, Mango. This question would require students to have (a) knowledge of English, (b) knowledge of the names for different kinds of fruit, and (c) reading skills. If these objects were rendered in pictures, however, then the question could be solved regardless of the language used by the student, no reading skill would be necessary, and no academic knowledge required.

An example of a Naglieri-V test item is provided in **figure 2.4**. In this question, the student needs to determine the similarities and differences among the six pictures. Students will notice that five of the images have some part that is round, two have a handle, two are brown, two are clear, one is filled, and all of them are used to contain something. What five of the pictures have in common is that they are empty, in contrast to the glass, which is not empty. Thus, the answer.

FIGURE 2.4 Example of a Naglieri-V Test Item

Nonverbal

The Naglieri General Ability Tests-Nonverbal (Naglieri-NV) measures general ability using questions that require a student to recognize the relationships among and attributes of shapes presented in, for example, a two-by-two or three-by-three orientation, often described as a progressive matrix. The nonverbal questions were constructed using patterns that form sequences and vary in their spatial orientations and other distinguishing characteristics that must be fully understood to determine the correct answer. The Naglieri-NV test items demand close examination of the relationships among the shapes included in each part of the matrix and the multiple-choice options. The ways the items are conceptualized and constructed vary, but they all require the student to determine what logic explains the relationships among the parts and which of five options completes the pattern.

An illustration of a typical nonverbal test item is shown in **figure 2.5**. To find the answer, the student needs to notice that the pattern of shapes changes across the rows (octagon, square, triangle), that the color of these shapes changes across the columns, and that a triangle is added inside the two shapes in the top two rows of the second column. By noticing these characteristics, students can arrive at the correct answer: 1.

This kind of test question is referred to as a nonverbal item because it is not necessary to identify a verbal concept to find the correct answer. Instead, the analogic relationship among the shapes drives the answer. The student's complete understanding of the logic is tested by the presentation of options that vary in the degree to which they are accurate. These items become very complex as the size of the matrix and the number of variables included increases.

FIGURE 2.5 Example of a Naglieri-NV Test Item

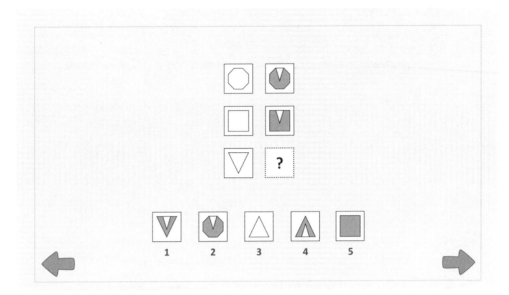

Quantitative

The Naglieri General Ability Tests-Quantitative (Naglieri-Q) items vary in their content, but all require close examination of the relationships among the numbers or symbols used to create every question. As in the verbal and nonverbal tests, in the Naglieri-Q, students must gain an understanding of the relationships among the numbers and symbols to identify which multiple-choice option answers the question.

The questions require the student to identify the equivalency of simple quantities, follow numerical sequences, and analyze a matrix of numbers. Minimal mathematical knowledge is required and calculation demands are simple. Item difficulty increases as the number of components increases, and the reasoning becomes more complex. None of the items are math word problems, allowing the student to solve each item regardless of the language they speak.

An example of a Naglieri-Q test item is presented in **figure 2.6**. In this example, the student needs to notice that the two parallelograms and two circles balance each other, as do the two hexagons on each side. Logically, then, one circle is equal to one parallelogram.

FIGURE 2.6. Example of a Naglieri Quantitative Test Item

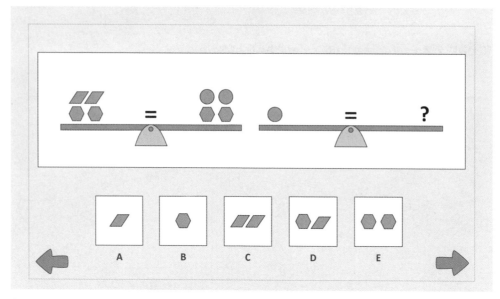

The descriptions of the three tests in the Naglieri battery illustrate their differences and similarities. They all require a student to fully understand relationships among pictures, shapes, or numbers to determine the correct answer. This is the essence of a test of general ability—to understand simple through complex relationships and sequences across many kinds of content. When the concept of general ability is described in this manner, its relationship to academic skills becomes clearer, since much of what students learn in school demands this kind of thinking.

Evidence for the Naglieri General Ability Tests

In part one, we have focused on two main points: the equity problem associated with gifted education and the role tests of ability have played in the underrepresentation of Black, Hispanic, and Native American students; English language learners; and students living in poverty. We have suggested that by removing the need for verbal instructions and verbal responses and by creating tests that can be solved regardless of the language(s) spoken by the student, greater equity can be achieved. There is, however, always the need for evidence to determine if this approach actually provides more equitable identification of students. The first study of these new measures has recently been completed.

Selvamenan et al. (2022) examined the utility of prepublication versions of the Naglieri General Ability Tests for 8,410 general-population students in grades preK–12. This study is a report of three separate investigations involving groups who received verbal,

By addressing the language and knowledge demands in the test items as well as in the directions and student responses, the Naglieri General Ability Tests appear to have helped achieve equity.

nonverbal, and quantitative test items. These tests had all the characteristics listed in this chapter and were administered on a computer. PreK students were tested in a one-on-one setting, kindergarteners in small groups of two or three students, and students in grades 1–12 in larger groups of up to ten students. The authors found trivial differences across race and ethnicity (as shown in **figure 2.3**), as well as across gender and parental education level, on the verbal, nonverbal, and quantitative tests. The results illustrate that by addressing the language and knowledge demands in the test items as well as in the directions and student responses, the Naglieri General Ability Tests appear to have helped achieve equity as evidenced by small mean score differences for students across race, ethnicity, and parental education level.

Chapter Summary

In this chapter we have shown the connections between the US Army Alpha and Beta and the origins of the tests typically used to measure ability for admission to gifted and talented educational programs. We have described how these tests' fundamental problem is the confounding impact prior academic knowledge has on the evaluation of ability. We have also described how, even though the men who initiated this approach recognized that tests that demand knowledge are unjust, these tests have, unfortunately, been widely used to the detriment of students of color, students learning English, and students living in poverty. We showed that the basic approach of measuring general ability using tests with verbal, nonverbal, and quantitative content can be improved. The several research studies presented show that by providing instructions using a video demonstration without words and by creating test questions that can be solved using any language and that don't demand prior academic knowledge, equity can be achieved across race, ethnicity, and parental education level.

PART TWO
Administering and Interpreting Ability Tests

CHAPTER

3
Logistical Considerations

Chapters 1 and 2 focused on the lack of equity within gifted education and the role tests of ability have played in underrepresentation in gifted programs, as well as what can be done to make these tests more equitable. In chapter 3, we discuss the test administration process and share suggestions for how schools can use test results. We present logistical issues and practical procedures associated with gifted testing and provide suggestions for successful implementation of testing in school and at home.

The Message Students Receive

A newborn is assessed at birth using an Apgar score that informs doctors and nurses of their health and immediate medical needs. So the cycle of testing begins . . . and continues throughout a person's lifetime. Prior to entering school, children participate in multiple assessments, both formal and informal. Most, if not all, are stressful. The testing environment, how a student prepares, and the outcome of each assessment depend on many factors, such as cultural norms and expectations, available resources, overall health, stress level, and test anxiety, to name a few. What stays consistent is the wish to do well: to make the team, to make parents proud or happy, to get the part, to pass the driver's test, to get into the desired university. In a world of high-stakes testing, students are often told of the importance of performing at the highest level—that their performance can change the trajectory of their lives. Whether or not this is true, it is also the message some students are given prior to testing for a gifted program. Regardless of the specific test being taken, we have witnessed students cry, hyperventilate, and shut down when it's time to "begin now." We would like to offer a gentler way of approaching gifted testing because the information shared with students matters, especially for students who have been marginalized and who may not feel as if they belong or are welcome in a gifted program.

We would like to offer a gentler way of approaching gifted testing because the information shared with students matters.

In his book *Tests and Measurement for People Who (Think They) Hate Tests and Measurement*, Salkind (2018) describes the purpose of testing: "In order for them [teachers and administrators] to take action to help the people [students] with whom they work, they need to first assess a particular behavior or set of behaviors. And to make that assessment, they use some kind of formal test . . . or informal test. . . . Then, based on their training and experience, they make a decision as to what course of action to take" (8). At the most basic level, educators test students so they can know how to help students. Test results help inform and direct necessary interventions so that appropriate measures can be put into place.

The information provided to students prior to taking a test for gifted services should be straightforward and simple. For students who have test anxiety, or those who are not fluent in English, lengthy test information is likely to be misunderstood, or not understood at all. Keeping it simple may help reduce anxiety and improve clarity around what is expected. We suggest test administrators use the following script, preferably in students' home languages, if possible, when providing students with information about the Naglieri General Ability Tests:

> *This is a different type of test than you may be used to, because it does not have any words in it. You are taking this test to help your teachers and parents understand how you think and learn. You will be looking at puzzles, pictures, symbols, and shapes to find patterns and relationships. This test will not be reflected as a grade or on a report card. We want to see how you think, not what you have learned in school.*

Test Administration: What You Need to Know

Educators routinely administer different types of tests, including formative and summative achievement tests. The following guidelines for preparing testing conditions can help test administrators make sure all students are prepared to do their best. These guidelines relate to test taking in general; they are not specific to gifted testing.

Testing Conditions

When administering any type of test, the test administrator plays a major role in creating the best possible test conditions. Test administrators cannot control how students come into the testing situation, but they can provide tips students and parents can follow to increase success and performance and reduce test anxiety.

Whether a student is trying out for a play or team or sitting for the SAT, share these common (and excellent) tips for success:

➤ Get a good night's rest the evening before the test.

➤ Eat a healthy meal before testing.

➤ Arrive early to the test location (or sign on a few minutes early if taking a test online).

➤ Bring water and stay hydrated during testing.

➤ Bring a non-sugary snack to the test, in case you get hungry.

➤ Before starting the test, take a few deep breaths. Deep breathing brings oxygen-rich blood to your brain, which helps it function optimally.

Some additional tips that are specific to testing for gifted services include the following:

➤ Read or examine each question carefully.

➤ Don't guess recklessly; look at all the answers to be sure which one you want to choose.

➤ Keep an eye on the time, and don't spend a lot of time on any one question because (some) tests have time limits.

➤ There is only one correct answer for each question.

➤ The questions start out easy and increase in difficulty throughout the test.

➤ If you get stuck, move on. If you have time once you finish the test, you can come back to any questions you skipped.

Deanna Shahverdian, the gifted testing technician for Paradise Valley Unified School District in Arizona, oversees close to three thousand assessments each year. She states, "Establishing best practices for test taking is important because students can only take a specific assessment [for gifted programming] once per year [in Arizona]. When families move into our district, some parents immediately request testing. I recommend that they wait until the student has established a routine in school [for a couple of weeks] before testing." Shahverdian believes that it is important for students to settle into school and experience a few normal school days before testing.

Prior to testing, check the school calendar to be sure no fire drill, "crazy hat" day, or other special events are scheduled. Gifted testing can be stressful for some students. Having everything else normal on testing day can help students better concentrate on the test itself.

Online Testing at School

For many years, schools throughout the country have been using online testing to identify students for gifted programs. There are tremendous advantages to online testing, including:

➤ no need to purchase physical copies of tests, which eliminates the need to store paper-and-pencil tests and maintain their security

➤ increased speed and accuracy for scoring

➤ ability to test more students during the testing window

➤ students' familiarity with technology can ease test anxiety

➤ increased student engagement in the test, since technology is more game-like

➤ reduced variables in testing conditions

➤ **Bonus!** It's good for the planet, and who doesn't want that?

Due to the COVID-19 pandemic, which kept many students from learning in person at school for a period of time, many school districts have begun utilizing online testing to assess students while at home. This type of online testing is discussed in further detail on page 38.

Test Administrators

Many schools and districts have classroom teachers administer gifted testing.* There are several advantages to this practice. Having teachers administer the test is often the most economical method, since staffing for additional test administrators is not needed. Classroom teachers can typically schedule testing over a two- or three-day time frame for all students in the grade level. This way, students who choose not to take the test can be supervised by one teacher at that grade level, who isn't administering testing. Another advantage is that students know their teachers. A familiar face during the test can often reduce test anxiety.

There are also disadvantages to using teachers as test administrators. Teachers may have an unintended bias with children they know, which might lead them to provide more support to students with whom they are familiar. Using classroom teachers to administer gifted testing can also greatly disrupt the school schedule.

Some districts use other staff or retired teachers as test administrators. This method can be more expensive, but it reduces the variables of testing and makes scheduling more convenient. It also allows for consistency of setup, builds a routine for test administration, and eases troubleshooting during and following the administration. Testing will likely still disrupt the schedule with this method; however, there will be less disruption overall.

---

*Although no specific training is required to administer the Naglieri General Ability Tests, it is best for teachers (or anyone administering the test) to familiarize themselves with the test and explicitly follow the directions in the administration manual.

Reducing Variables

To ensure test results are valid, it is important to reduce variables in test administration. Ideally, testing should take place in the morning, at the same time each day, and in the same place.

To prepare the test environment, test administrators must:

➤ Check the school calendar to make sure no fire drill or other special events are scheduled and no construction is taking place. Machinery can be very distracting to students!

➤ Post signs on the door and in the hallway informing people that testing is underway.

➤ Inform the school office that testing is taking place to reduce interruptions in the classroom.

➤ Check students' cell phones at the door. And make sure their own phones are turned off or set to silent mode.

➤ Encourage students to bring water bottles, but make sure they are clear and without a label.

➤ Ensure scratch paper and pencils are available.

Special Considerations and Testing Accommodations

Special considerations for testing should be given to students in certain groups. These include students with Individualized Education Programs (IEP) or 504 Accommodation Plans, English language learners, and students who live in poverty. The Naglieri General Ability Tests do not include verbal directions or words, which may mitigate or reduce some testing challenges. But testing accommodations on a student's IEP or 504 plan must be followed. **Figure 3.1** describes some common testing accommodations and solutions when using the Naglieri General Ability Tests.

Along with the accommodations recommended in **figure 3.1**, the following list includes additional ideas to support specific groups.

➤ **English language learners.** Integral to the development of the Naglieri General Ability Tests are test items that are solvable in any language. Verbal comprehension has been removed from the instructions, and verbal expression from the responses. Directions may also be administered in Spanish.

➤ **Twice-exceptional (2e) students.** Although the Naglieri General Ability Tests were not developed or specifically studied for relevance to 2e students—gifted students who also have a learning or other disability—the simple instructional videos are animated and language free, which can help 2e students easily understand the test-taking directions.

➤ **Culturally diverse students.** The verbal test uses universally recognized pictures appropriate across cultures that represent verbal concepts, rather than presenting questions orally. The nonverbal and quantitative tests use shapes and numbers which are universally recognized.

FIGURE 3.1 Common Accommodations and Solutions for the Naglieri General Ability Tests

Accommodation*	Solutions
Use color overlays.	Color overlays make text easier to read. Since the Naglieri General Ability Tests do not include any text, overlays are not necessary. Colors used on the nonverbal test can be used with colorblind students. The colors used to render test items were selected to be appropriate for use with students with limited visual capability. Test questions can be magnified.
Allow extra time.	The amount of extra time can be determined by the test administrator.
Use computer for testing.	An online version of the test is available.
Use a prompter.	If a prompter is needed, the student can indicate an answer verbally and the prompter can input the answers on the computer.
Have someone scribe to write and capture responses.	Online testing is available with no need to scribe.
Provide larger items or use magnification for visually impaired students.	Larger images can be provided for the tests.
Break up the test and allow frequent breaks.	Test sections of the Naglieri General Ability Tests may be separated to provide necessary breaks.
Allow preferential seating.	The online testing format allows for multiple seating scenarios.
Administer exam in a place without distractions.	This is a common practice for all ability testing scenarios.

∗ Common accommodations noted here are derived from Cambridge Assessment International Education (2021).

Online Testing at Home

Online testing at home began prior to the COVID-19 pandemic in 2020, but it was primarily used for individual testing of students who were homebound, home schooled, or had other accommodation needs. During the pandemic, schools around the globe had to pivot rapidly to online testing for large numbers of students. This was problematic for most schools and presented a considerable challenge for schools with limited resources.

Schools that already had one-to-one technology and online learning in place were able to make the transition much earlier and more successfully than underresourced schools that had limited or no technological devices for students to use at home. This not only had immediate effects, but it also continues to perpetuate the issue of diversity in gifted programs.

The immediate effects were obvious: students could not get online for school, and as a result they had learning loss in much greater proportions than students who were able to pivot immediately to online learning.

The longer-term effects are beginning to show in recent reports published by the Office for Civil Rights (2021). Annual achievement testing across the country has yielded significant evidence of learning loss due to school closures during the pandemic. For students who already had a learning gap, the loss of access and opportunities has widened it. Students of color are even further behind than they were before the pandemic, as are English language learner students who had the dual challenge of learning content and English. Now, add to this dilemma the way these effects can impact students' intellectual scores on traditional ability tests that have knowledge-based test questions. Access and resources are unavailable, resulting in lower achievement, which is reflected on ability test scores. The cycle continues.

Whatever the reasons for online testing at home, the practice has advantages and disadvantages. For students with test anxiety, testing in their home environment can be more comfortable and can reduce anxious feelings. The same may be true for marginalized students who are invisible to educators and underrepresented in gifted programs, plus testing at home can allow for additional support for both students and parents. It also gives all families greater flexibility by providing options to test in the evening or on weekends.

There are also some disadvantages to this method. At-home testing is often difficult or impossible for students from lower-income households. Even if schools provide one-to-one devices, some students may not have an internet connection or have an unreliable one. While many school districts provide internet connection devices for students who need them, they are often not available to all in need. Even when these resources are made available, parents may not be at home to support the child if problems occur during the testing.

In contrast, affluent families usually have secure and consistent internet connectivity, making it easier to gather information, such as testing dates and times. Also, in higher income households, there may be a parent who does not work or is easily able to take time off or work from home, making it more likely that an adult will be available to assist the child with online learning and assessments. However, that can also lead to parents aiding children by helping to answer test questions during the test. Despite their best intentions, it may be difficult for some parents to refrain from assisting their children. If it is found that parents assisted students with answers during the test, the test will be invalidated, and the student may need to take a different, additional test.

For the purpose of identifying gifted students, it is imperative that we have an accurate portrayal of the students' abilities to solve the test items independently. To address this concern, we recommend parents agree to testing conditions, such as those presented in the reproducible form on page 40.

To help mitigate inequities, we suggest providing support for students testing at home in the form of an initial "getting ready" session. For example, Shahverdian describes the procedures she follows using her school district's adopted platforms, Google Meet and Google Classroom, for at-home testing. Prior to the test date, and under the supervision of the test administrator, students practice logging into the testing site where they input exam codes and student identification information. The test administrator defines expectations for students, and students practice how they can get help, if needed, during the assessment. During this session, Shahverdian verifies that the student's WiFi is able to run Google Meet along with the testing platform. By including a "getting ready" session, test administrators can see which students are already tech savvy and which may need more help prior to administering the actual test. This session may also help alleviate some anxiety for students, parents, and test administrators.

Practicing in advance is helpful since most problems that arise during testing involve technology. During a "getting ready" session, it helps to have someone available who can troubleshoot, both at school and at home. This brief practice session helps prepare students, parents, and test administrators to ensure optimal testing conditions. You can also share the reproducible on page 42 that provides some reminders and tips for remote gifted testing.

> For the purpose of identifying gifted students, it is imperative that we have an accurate portrayal of the students' abilities to solve the test items independently. To address this concern, we recommend parents agree to testing conditions. To help mitigate inequities, we suggest providing support for students testing at home in the form of an initial "getting ready" session.

Terms and Conditions for At-Home Testing

Parents (or legal guardians) and students, by signing this document, you agree to these terms:

- The test instructions, items, practice items, and answers remain secure and confidential. Photographs, photocopies, screen captures, verbal discussions, written comments, and other reproduction of any portion of the assessment are NOT permitted—before, during, or after testing. Each of the foregoing is considered a breach of copyright and will be treated as such.
- Tests are to be taken only by the assigned student.
- Students are not to receive assistance on tests from any individual or resource (textbook, internet site, cell phone texting, etc.) while testing.
- Tests are not to be viewed by anyone other than the assigned student.
- If a student has a 504 or IEP, test accommodations are strictly followed.

Requirements for Completing Testing

- Students are required to have their cameras on for the duration of the testing.
- Students are required to wear headphones to take the test. (Headphones will be provided to the student if needed.)
- Students must be alone in the testing room while completing the test.
- Cell phones, smart watches, calculators, or any other electronic devices that are not being used in the testing administration are not to be in the student's workspace.

Students may be required to take an additional, different assessment should these test results be invalidated due to the following conditions:

- The student did not follow the procedures and requirements described above.
- The student was assisted during the testing in a manner that was not specifically permitted.
- Possible interference during the student's testing as observed through remote proctoring.

Determining whether a student needs to retake a test is at the sole discretion of the school administration.

Testing terms and conditions created by Deanna Shahverdian, 2021. Used with permission.

From *Understanding and Using the Naglieri General Ability Tests: A Call for Equity in Gifted Education* by Dina Brulles, Ph.D., Kimberly Lansdowne, Ph.D., and Jack A. Naglieri, Ph.D., copyright © 2022. This page may be reproduced for individual, classroom, or small group work only. For all other uses, contact Free Spirit Publishing at freespirit.com/permissions.

Confirmation of Agreement

My signature below confirms that:

- I am the parent or legal guardian of the student.
- I am the student taking the test.
- I consent to my child participating in the remote administration of the testing using the platforms and processes specified by district administration.
- l have fully read, understand, and agree to abide by the above terms and conditions regarding test security and testing practices and understand that they apply to my child and to myself.
- I understand and agree to follow all policies and procedures specified for this assessment.

Parent/Guardian Name (Please print): _____

Student Name (Please print): _____

Parent Signature: _____Date: _____

Student Signature: _____Date: _____

Important Reminders and Tips for At-Home Testing

General Guidelines for Testing

- Parents may help with login, if necessary.
- Parents MAY NOT ASSIST students with answers in any way.
- Parents should contact the school administration for help with technical issues.

Setting Up the Testing Environment

- Create a comfortable testing space that includes a desk or table for the student.
- Remove distractions.
- Turn off TVs, music, and other distracting noises.
- Plan sibling activities away from the testing space.
- Ensure that when testing has started, your child is in a room without distractions, pets, or other people.

The Day of Testing

- Ensure that the computer is plugged in or has been fully charged, and that the charger is nearby if needed.
- Check audio sound, headphones, earbuds, and/or speakers.
- Turn off other devices using the internet, including video games and streaming services, to ensure minimal activity on the home network.
- Have student testing session code and ID on a notecard to ease check-in.

During Testing

- Turn the student's camera on for digital monitoring during testing.
- Test administrators communicate and take questions as needed.
- Students and the test administrator use the "Chat" option to communicate and troubleshoot as needed.

Test Prep Advice

We often hear about parents "prepping" their children for ability tests. Educators with experience administering these tests have noted concerns from students who claim they have been "practicing" using questions or items that are similar (or even the same) as those encountered on the actual tests. It is important to recognize that while the student may have seen items like those in the Naglieri General Ability Tests, what determines the score is the student's ability to fully understand the relationships among the pictures or numbers provided in the test questions and to decide which option among several, some of which are partially correct, is the answer.

Some commercial test prep guides may inhibit student performance when taking tests since students who have been previously exposed to test items sometimes feel overly confident. When this occurs, they may rush through the test without taking the time to carefully consider what each item is asking. This familiarity greatly increases the likelihood of test error, and despite good intentions by parents, is often disadvantageous to students.

Remember, the goal is to test students' true intellectual ability, not their learned knowledge. Therefore, we discourage the use of prepared materials to practice test *content*. However, we do encourage general test-taking preparation, since the kind of abstract questions presented on an ability test may be very new to students. You can share these tips with parents who want to set children up for success on an ability test:

> We discourage the use of prepared materials to practice test *content*. However, we do encourage general test-taking preparation, since the kind of abstract questions presented on an ability test may be very new to students.

- ➤ Explain that it is important for the student to look at the questions carefully.

- ➤ Explain that the questions will increase in difficulty throughout the test.

- ➤ Practice sitting still and attending to a task for twenty to thirty minutes at a time.

- ➤ Remind students that while there are several choices, only one answer is correct.

- ➤ Teach students how to work through the process of elimination, as these tests involve multiple-choice questions.

- ➤ Make sure students are physically comfortable (this includes their seating option, visual display, hunger, bathroom needs, etc.).

Sharing Test Results with Parents and Teachers

School personnel take different approaches when sharing test results with parents and teachers. It is important to know what your state's gifted mandate dictates and what, if anything, is supported by school district policy. If no policy exists that prescribes what specific information should be shared with parents and teachers, then best practice would maintain that a school administrative team work together to determine the level of specificity to include when reporting test results.

Sharing Information with Parents

Once testing is complete, it's time to inform parents of their children's test scores. This can be challenging for many reasons. Parents may have strong reactions—positive and negative—to the identification. They may not know what test scores mean, or what to do with the information. Gifted services may be uncharted territory for some families who may not understand or be aware of these programs. In addition to sending out written materials about a student's test score, we suggest holding both in-person and online meetings explaining the gifted services offered, the logistics of the program, and an overview of the meaning behind an ability test and scores. Building relationships with parents is crucial to student success. And the more information you provide, the more buy-in you will get from families. An additional challenge when reporting scores is explaining *how* scores are interpreted and used.

These considerations, including national and local norms, which are introduced in the parent letters on pages 45 and 47, are described in detail in chapter 4. The letters may be used to share a student's results on the Naglieri General Ability Tests with parents. Each contains similar information, but they differ in *how* the information may be used.

The letter on page 45 describes results that are determined by comparing a student to other students locally, in the same grade, school, or district (also called a local norm). Using universal testing, a school district may use local norms to find the top X percent of students in their community whom they've determined need specialized services. In this situation, the need for special services depends not so much on a student's standing relative to age- or grade-mates nationally, but on the student's standing relative to the other students in their class, school, or district. Since these are *local* comparisons, portability of identification cannot be confirmed. If a family moves to another district or school, identification and programming may not continue. The second letter describes scores comparing a student's standing relative to age- or grade-mates nationally. Since these are national scores, families who move *may* transport these scores to new districts.

Date: _____

Dear Parent(s)/Guardian(s):

In an ongoing effort to gather information to guide curriculum and instruction for our students, _____ [school/school district] tests all _____ graders each year to determine the need for specialized advanced academic services that best meet students' individual needs.

_____ [student name] recently participated in this universal testing and completed the Naglieri General Ability Tests, which measure thinking with verbal, nonverbal, and quantitative test content. The questions on these three tests measure a student's general ability to understand relationships among pictures (the verbal test), diagrams (the nonverbal test), and numbers (the quantitative test). The questions on these tests can be solved regardless of what language a student speaks and the tests do not require knowledge taught in school.

The test scores provided below are percentile scores. It is important to note that a percentile is not the same as the percent of questions answered correctly. Percentile scores provide a comparison of your child's performance to our local community. Percentile scores are used to rank students on a scale of 1 to 99. If a student has a percentile of 71, it indicates this student scored higher than 70 of every 100 students that took the same test at _____ [school/school district]. If your child scores in the top 10 percent of students at _____ [school/school district], specialized services are necessary.

Here are your child's Naglieri General Ability Tests results:

Verbal _____ percentile

Nonverbal _____ percentile

Quantitative _____ percentile

For purposes of universal testing, _____ [school/school district] is using local norms to determine the top _____ percent of students who need specialized advanced academic services in this community. This is important because the need for special services depends not so much on a student's standing relative to age- or grade-mates nationally, but on the student's standing relative to the other students in the class, school, or district.

Since these are *local* scores, they may not apply in other districts. If you move to another district, your child's scores may not qualify them for specialized services or they may have to be tested again. For more information on the Naglieri General Ability Tests, please visit the website mhs.com/info/gthub.

For information about advanced academic services, test scores, and what you can expect for your child, please join us for a meeting at _____ on _____ [location and date] at _____ [time] or online on _____ [date] at _____ [time]. You can also visit our website at _____ [school/school district website].

Sincerely,

[your name and title]

Date: _____

Dear Parent(s)/Guardian(s):

For purposes of qualifying for advanced academic services, _____ [student name] recently completed the Naglieri General Ability Tests, which measure thinking with verbal, nonverbal, and quantitative test content. The questions on these tests measure a student's general ability to understand relationships among pictures (the verbal test), diagrams (the nonverbal test), and numbers (the quantitative test). The questions on these tests can be solved regardless of what language a student speaks and do not require knowledge taught in school.

The test scores provided below are percentile scores. It is important to note that a percentile is not the same as the percent of questions answered correctly. Percentile scores provide a comparison of your child's performance to that of a national sample of students the same age. Percentile scores are used to rank students on a scale of 1 to 99. If a student has a percentile of 71, it indicates this student scored higher than 70 of every 100 students that took the same test nationally. If your child scores in the top 3 percent of students in the nation, specialized services are necessary.

Here are your child's Naglieri General Ability Tests results:

Verbal _____ percentile

Nonverbal _____ percentile

Quantitative _____ percentile

For more information on the Naglieri General Ability Tests, please visit mhs.com/info/gthub.

For information about advanced academic services, test scores, and what you can expect for your child, please join us for a meeting at _____ on _____ [location and date] at _____ [time] or online on _____ [date] at _____ [time]. You can also visit our website at _____ [school/school district website].

Sincerely,

[your name and title]

Sharing Information with Teachers

Practices for sharing student test results with teachers vary widely. Some district-level administrators feel that teachers need to be aware of the test results so they can meet the needs of the students in their classrooms. The purpose of testing is to inform educators about the learning needs of their students. Therefore, it seems logical to share the results with teachers, since the information can help guide instruction in ways that maximize student learning. However, teachers need support in understanding what the tests measure, how to interpret the results, and how to use that information.

The definitions for levels of giftedness can differ, but they have some commonality among the experts. An IQ score in the range of 115–129 is generally described as bright, an IQ score in the range of 130–144 is generally described as gifted, and an IQ score of 145 or higher is generally described as highly or profoundly gifted. **Figure 3.2** shows the levels of giftedness and the normal distribution of IQ test scores. Knowing a student's level of giftedness can help inform educators about that student's potential and guide the discussion about programming.

> Teachers need support in understanding what the tests measure, how to interpret the results, and how to use that information.

FIGURE 3.2 Levels of Giftedness and Normal Distribution of IQ Test Scores

Level	Ability Score	Ratio to Total Population
Bright	115–129	1:30
Gifted	130–144	1:40–1:1,000
Highly gifted	145–159	1:1,000–1:10,000
Profoundly gifted	160+	1:10,000–1:1 million

A student's level of ability greatly impacts the type of instruction, the educational placement, and the supports the student needs. Students at the *bright* level can generally be appropriately challenged within the regular classroom with some modifications to their curriculum. Students at this level are likely to find intellectual peers with whom they can interact.

Students at the *gifted* level may also be sufficiently challenged in a regular classroom, especially when the gifted students are clustered together into one gifted cluster class at each grade level.* Students at this level are also more likely to feel accepted by other gifted students in their cluster classroom setting, especially when the gifted students are grouped together in the classroom.

---

*For this grouping to be effective, the cluster teacher needs to participate in ongoing professional learning opportunities in gifted education and must be able to differentiate the curriculum and instruction for the gifted students placed in the class. See chapter 5 for additional information on cluster grouping.

Students at the *highly gifted* and *profoundly gifted* levels require dramatically different curriculum and instruction than other students their age. These students benefit from opportunities for radical acceleration in areas where they are highly achieving and academically advanced. Highly and profoundly gifted learners typically thrive on opportunities to self-direct their learning, build on areas of interest and expertise, and study concepts in greater depth and with more complexity. These students require a more personalized approach that is not bound by grade-level limitations.

Regardless of their educational placement and level of giftedness, gifted students share a few basic traits. They learn at a much faster pace than others, they process information to a much greater depth, and they demonstrate higher levels of intensity, imagination, and intellectual ability. They are also likely to show heightened sensitivity and emotions. For these reasons, they need curriculum, instruction, and understanding outside the norm in order to learn. And they need teachers who understand their unique traits and associated learning needs.

Given the wide range of ability levels associated with gifted learners, it is helpful for teachers to consider general characteristics of gifted children. With this understanding, teachers can then differentiate among the varying levels of giftedness and modify instructional approaches accordingly.

Sharing Information with Students: A Parent's Decision

A question commonly asked by both parents and teachers is: "Should students know their scores on ability tests?" Sharing this information with students is a personal choice that the student's family decides how to address. Many educators believe it is important that students know and understand their unique learning needs so they can advocate for themselves. And many gifted students inherently understand that their learning needs differ from their age peers, since grade-level curriculum is often not new or challenging for them. Some students may even take an online IQ test of their own accord, but are then left to interpret the results without any perspective on what they mean.

There are pros and cons associated with telling students their specific score. If students don't understand the meaning of their scores, having this information can sometimes lead to other issues, such as imposter syndrome ("Maybe I don't really belong here."), intellectual arrogance, and unreasonable pressure to be "perfect." On the other hand, knowing and understanding their score can bolster self-esteem, encourage intellectual stimulation, and provide answers for why a student might feel so different from peers. Parents must ultimately make the decision on how much information to share with their child. Educators can provide the following talking points for parents who choose to share scores with their children to help guide the discussion:

➤ Share the student's score and what it means. ("You scored in the 130–144 range. This means that you scored higher than ninety-five out of one hundred kids your age.")

- Share that the score shows the student has learning needs that are different from those of their classmates and they will need different classwork and activities to meet their needs.

- Remind students that their score doesn't mean they won't have to work hard in their classes.

- Share the areas the student excelled in and explain that this means they will need different work from classmates in these areas.

If a child has questions about what giftedness means, parents can share *The Survival Guide for Gifted Kids* by Judy Galbraith with kids ages ten and under. Teens can read *The Gifted Teen Survival Guide* by Judy Galbraith and Jim Delisle.

Chapter Summary

Chapter 3 presented logistical ideas to assist educators in planning and preparing for at-home and in-school gifted testing. We provided guidelines and tips to share with students and families prior to gifted tested and considerations for sharing the results with teachers, parents, and students. In chapter 4, we turn to what transpires after testing happens.

4
Understanding and Using Test Scores

In this chapter we discuss what happens after the testing process.* We offer a variety of ways to consider and use the test scores, including methods for using local and national norms and suggestions for implementation.

Screening Versus Identification

We are often asked if a short test, or screener, should be used to identify students for more thorough testing, or a second round of testing. In essence, a screening measure could be used in conjunction with testing, creating a two-step identification process. However, using a two-step identification process begs these questions:

➤ Is a two-step process really necessary?

➤ What possible benefits and outcomes can be derived from a two-step approach?

➤ How would a two-step identification process impact diversity, equity, and inclusion in gifted programs?

➤ How does the validity of the screening test compare to the validity of the complete test?

These questions lead us to perhaps the most important consideration: For what are students being screened (or tested)? In short, we are seeking to identify students so that we can help determine their most appropriate and beneficial instruction to ensure that the services students receive fit their needs. When

---

*Once testing is complete, the data needs to be reviewed and interpreted by someone with knowledge of psychometrics. This is usually a coordinator of gifted services or testing coordinator for the district. It is common for teachers to administer ability tests, but interpretation and analysis should be done by someone with specific training in testing and measurement.

considering assessment tools and procedures, it is critical to consider your gifted program's objectives and services. Most districts develop a gifted program, test for identification, and *then* place students into that program.

On the face of it, this process seems logical. But if we are identifying students whose academic needs are so advanced that they need different curriculum and activities from their peers, shouldn't we first determine these students' needs and then develop programs tailored to them? We recognize that this sounds like a chicken-and-egg dilemma, but we believe that the program or services being offered should be determined *after* identifying students and their needs.

We believe that the program or services being offered should be determined *after* identifying students and their needs.

If a program already exists, and the district is resistant to modifying services, it is important to select measures that are consistent with the programs available for students. For example, a student shows quantitative reasoning skills far beyond that of the other students being tested. To meet their full potential, this student needs access to services that address this ability. However, the only services available are an advanced reading group and a drama enrichment program. While these services may contribute to the student's social skills by allowing them to participate in a group activity with peers, they do not meet the student's academic needs.

The flip side to this issue is that many districts do not have a dedicated gifted program. However, even if a district doesn't have a formal program and services, ability testing should still take place. Scores on these tests provide classroom teachers with a range of the abilities in their classroom, grade level, school, or district, and help them determine how to best serve all their students. Students who score at the top, even if there is no formal gifted program, still benefit from strategies such as acceleration in particular subject areas, grouping for instruction, and other modifications that meet their advanced needs.

In districts that have gifted programs, objectives need to be clear and well developed to serve the needs of gifted students. It is important for schools to create programs that are sustainable and that serve their students and their communities. Chapters 5 and 6 provide information on creating gifted services that respond to student needs.

Some districts use screening tools as a first round in the identification process. We do not recommend this practice. Screening tools, such as rating scales, can be used with ability tests, but they should not be used to decide which students will be given an ability test nor to identify giftedness on their own. Using screening tests in these ways contributes to the underrepresentation of some groups in gifted programs, since it represents an extra hurdle to identification. An ability test that is designed to identify gifted students can take the place of a screening test. When the Naglieri General Ability Tests are administered to all students in a school or grade level, they serve as an identification tool that gives every student the opportunity to be identified.

Another common issue that contributes to underrepresentation in gifted programs is when districts use ability tests in conjunction with other tests, especially tests of achievement, for the purpose of gifted identification. If a student scores, for example, in the top 8 percent on a valid test of general ability, they should not have to again prove that they qualify for gifted programming by taking a second test. Most tests used in schools are developed for a singular purpose, whether that be to measure ability or achievement. An achievement test does not measure general ability, and should not be used in identifying gifted students, on its own or paired with an ability test, since these methods contribute to inequities in gifted programs, as discussed in part one.

The Naglieri General Ability Tests were designed as standalone measures. Requiring that students meet multiple measures with different types of tests can defeat the intended outcome of any one of the measures and perpetuate the underrepresentation of certain populations.

A good example of the importance of the logic used to aggregate data to arrive at an eligibility decision for students to be included in a gifted program is found in the ruling of *McFadden vs. Board of Education for Illinois School District U-46* (2013; 984 F.Supp.2d 882). Even though Hispanic students made up approximately 40 percent of the population of the district, only 2 percent of the students in the district's gifted program were Hispanic. Parents claimed that the school district failed to eliminate language barriers in violation of the Equal Educational Opportunities Act (EEOA) and that this limited Hispanic students' and English language learners' educational benefits in violation of federal and state constitutions.

The district was using the Naglieri Nonverbal Ability Test to identify students with high ability, but they had an additional requirement for entrance into the district's gifted program that caused the underrepresentation of Hispanic students. The additional requirement, that students attain high scores on a measure of ability that demanded knowledge of English and academic math skills, denied access to students who did not speak English fluently or had limited academic achievement. The judge ruled that the tests that demanded knowledge of English excluded Hispanic students from the gifted program because gifted children for whom English is a second language would likely score lower on the verbal and quantitative tests than the Naglieri Nonverbal Ability Test. The Naglieri General Ability Tests were developed to eliminate the demand of knowledge and linguistic skills in determining the need for advanced academic services.

Universal Testing

In recent years, there has been a strong movement toward universal testing in schools, which stems from a desire to increase gifted identification in underidentified, underrepresented, and underserved populations. Sometimes referred to as blanket testing, universal testing describes the systematic assessment of *all* students within a grade level for the purpose of identifying students with exceptional ability or potential. This method can be especially useful in finding gifted students from underrepresented populations, including Black, Hispanic, and Native American students; English language learners; and students living in poverty. Universal testing can help schools identify their students who are performing beyond grade-level peers, or have the potential to do so, and who need more or significantly different academic services than their age-mates. Bright students who may need some differentiation of instruction may also be found using universal screening or testing.

National and Local Norms

Equitable representation in gifted programs is affected not only by the type of tests used for identification, but also by how these tests are used (Peters and Engerand 2016) and by the very definition of gifted students. The National Association for Gifted Children (2019) states, "Students with gifts and talents perform—or have the capability to perform—at higher levels compared to others of the same age, experience, and environment in one or more domains." This comparison to "others of the same age" can be accomplished using a national or local point of reference.

National norms compare a student's performance to a sample of students of the same age or grade across the country who have been tested using the same measure. The sample of students used to create a national norm should be sufficiently large (i.e., thousands of students) and similar to the country's demographics across important variables such as age, gender, race, ethnicity, parental educational level (socioeconomic status), and location (urban, suburban, or rural) (AERA, APA, NCME 2014). Any published test that yields scores based on a normative sample should provide detailed information about just how similar that sample is to the composition of the country.

Local norms are used when a student's scores are compared to students in a similar group (i.e., all students in a particular grade in a school or school district). As with a national norm, the sample of students used to create a local norm should be sufficiently large and similar to the local demographics across important variables. As explained by many education organizations, "Local norms are often useful in conjunction with published [national] norms, especially if the local population differs markedly from the population on which published norms are based. In some cases local norms may be used exclusively" (AERA, APA, NCME 2014, 196).

These two methods of norming answer different but equally important questions: *What score does a student earn in relation to a representative sample of students of the same age across the country?* and *What score does a student earn in relation to their local community?*

Both national and local norms are used in the field of gifted education in the United States. National norms are appropriate when the demographic composition of the school or district resembles the US population. However, in areas where a school's or district's population differs markedly from the national population, local norms are more useful since they compare a student's score to a sample of students that more precisely reflects the characteristics of the community.

When using local norms, administrators responsible for identifying students for gifted programs can choose to create norms based on:

➤ the performance of all students in the same grade across the school district

➤ the performance of all students in the same grade within the same school or a subgroup of schools

➤ the performance of all students in the same grade within the same school

Whether you use national or local norms, comparison to "others of the same age" should identify the students who need additional services to meet their needs. The decision to use national or local norms should be made only after a careful consideration of equity.

Local Norming Process Using the Naglieri General Ability Tests

The following steps describe the basic process for developing local norms. We begin with a brief overview, and then more detail follows. These steps are, of course, general, and not all possible implications are presented, only the essential ones.

Step 1: Select a test or combination of tests to use. Select which combination of the Naglieri General Ability Tests-Verbal (Naglieri-V), -Nonverbal (Naglieri-NV), and -Quantitative (Naglieri-Q) are to be administered. Assessment procedures require an allocation of limited resources, most specifically time and money, which can limit the number of tests administered in a given year. These limitations highlight the importance of choosing the best test for the school or district student population. In determining the best combination of tests, keep in mind these questions:

➤ What is the goal of identification?

➤ What are your state's requirements?

➤ Does your state have a published list of tests that can be used?

The Naglieri General Ability Tests can be used in any combination to meet (most) state requirements for gifted identification, as well as the goals of local school administrators. In some schools and school districts, the tests may be used as part of a larger assessment process to make decisions about eligibility for gifted programs. It is important to consider the implications of how information from other measures, such as rating scales, observations, grades, and so on, will be used in the identification process.

Step 2: Test all your students. Local norming of the Naglieri General Ability Tests demands that all students are tested to obtain a reference point that represents the community. That is, creating a local norm against which all students are compared must include *all* students, not just those referred by teachers or parents or those who were part of some initial screening. Creating a local norm using universal testing eliminates the need for an initial screening test because the local norming process serves both a screening and an identification function.

Step 3: Interpret the data. Interpretation of the data obtained for local norming in a district is accomplished by calculating several kinds of scores. The most basic score is the total number of questions answered correctly. This is commonly called a raw score. (For definitions of this and other testing terms, see **figure 4.1.**) The raw score is then used to calculate other scores, such as percentile ranks and standard scores, that aid interpretation. The various scores are more fully explained later in this chapter.

Step 4: Determine the cut score. Decide on a cut score that will be used to suggest inclusion in the gifted program. Questions to consider when deciding on a cut score include:

> ➤ How many seats are available in the gifted program? *If the number is small, consider a higher cut score, say the 95th percentile. If there are many seats to fill, consider a cut score of the 92nd percentile.*

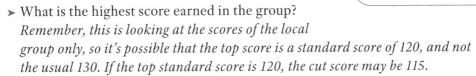

Creating a local norm against which all students are compared must include *all* students.

> ➤ What is the highest score earned in the group? *Remember, this is looking at the scores of the local group only, so it's possible that the top score is a standard score of 120, and not the usual 130. If the top standard score is 120, the cut score may be 115.*

> ➤ What is the range of scores in the group? *If the range is great, they could be put into stanines, or groups, and the cut score could be in the top two groups.*

One of the benefits of using local norms is that cut scores may be determined by the local administration.

Step 5: Decide how to weight assessment data. Decide how to combine the various scores used in the assessment process in relation to district goals and resources. Many districts, in addition to test scores, use other identification tools such as teacher ratings, student portfolios, and achievement data. *If* multiple measures are being considered, to ensure equity, it may be desirable to weight each data point. An example of this in a district or school that uses both ability test scores and teacher ratings to determine eligibility might be that ability test scores count twice as much as teacher ratings.

Another thing to consider is whether high test scores are required on all or only some of the measures obtained. For example, if a student scores at the 97th percentile of the verbal portion, does that student also need to score at this level on the nonverbal and quantitative portions, or can they receive services based on the one score? Another one of the many advantages of using local norms is the district's ability to determine if and how measures are weighted.

Reporting Local Norms

There are several kinds of scores that can be used when reporting local norms including local standard scores, local percentile rank, local stanines, and local rank order. This decision is generally made by the district or school administrator who oversees gifted education. Scores are designated as "local" when they are determined using a local norming method. See the definitions in figure 4.1 for an overview of these scores, which are described in the sections that follow.

Testing Terms and Definitions

Next, we define common testing terms. **Figure 4.1** provides an overview of the terms for quick reference. Key terms are described in detail in the sections that follow.

FIGURE 4.1 Testing Terms and Definitions

Testing Term	Definition
Raw score	This score represents the number of questions answered correctly on a test.
Rank order	Rank order represents a student's placement, from lowest to highest, using their raw score.
Percentile*	A score that varies from 0 (lowest score) to 99.9 (highest score) and is interpreted as follows: the student did as well as or better than X percent of the comparison group.
Z score	This score is calculated from the raw score and set so that the average is 0 and 68 percent of people earn a score between -1 and +1.
Standard score	This score is made from the Z score and typically set so that the average score is 100 and 68 percent of people earn a score between 85 and 115.
Standard deviation	The standard deviation is the size of the deviation from the mean that includes 68 percent of the group.
Stanine	One of nine equal segments in a normal distribution: ■ 1, 2, and 3 are below average ■ 4, 5, and 6 are average ■ 7, 8, and 9 are above average
National norms	When a large, nationally representative sample of people have taken a test, the raw scores can be converted to the scores noted above so that any person who takes the same test can be compared to the other people of the same age in the country.
Local norms	When a large enough sample of people in a local community have taken a test, the raw scores can be converted to the scores noted above so that any other person who takes the same test can be compared to the typical person of the same age in the local community.

*The score most often used for reporting test results

Raw Score

The number of correct answers on a test is called a raw score, and it is the starting point for any test interpretation. The raw score is typically computed by adding all the items answered correctly up to the point where some discontinue rule has been met. For the Naglieri General Ability Tests, the discontinue rule is set at four consecutive items answered incorrectly. Any responses to items that were given after the four consecutive incorrect items are not scored. This approach is used because a multiple-choice test gives students the opportunity to select the correct score by chance (e.g., 20 percent when there are five options) and not by actually solving the problem, which introduces measurement error into the score that is obtained.

Raw scores are used to create other types of scores when using local or national norms. To aid interpretation, the raw score is typically converted to other scores such as the percentile rank, standard score, and stanine.

Local Rank Order

Local rank order is used to identify students with the highest raw scores. A student's local rank order describes their raw score in comparison to the raw scores of the local reference group that consists of same-grade peers who have taken the same form of the same test. Each student's raw score is given a rank between 1 (denoting the highest raw score) and the maximum rank possible within that sample (the lowest raw score) based on the number of students within the selected sample. For example, in a local norm sample that consists of sixty third-grade students within a school building, students' raw scores would be ranked from 1 (highest raw score) to 60 (lowest raw score). Students with the same raw score are given the same rank order. If three students score a 1, the next rank is 4, as shown in **figure 4.3**.

The local rank order provides a way to easily evaluate the relative standing of each student's score in comparison to the group of same-grade peers. Local rank order can be used to identify, for example, the top 10 percent of students who could be considered for gifted programming.

Local Standard Score

A local standard score is another way to compare a student's score to a local norm sample. Local standard scores are based on a comparison between a student's raw score and scores obtained from students of the same grade in the local norm sample. This score can be obtained using the student's raw score, the average raw score of the sample (the mean), and the standard deviation of the raw scores for the local norm group at each grade. It is determined using this formula: *local standard score =((raw score - mean) / standard deviation) x 15 + 100*. The resulting value describes the distance a student's raw score is above or below the mean score of the local norm sample.

The local standard score provides a way of describing students using scores like those typically provided with nationally normed standardized tests where a score of, for example, 120 (90th percentile) would suggest the student would likely be appropriate for a gifted education program. These scores may or may not be the same as those obtained when compared to a national norm. For better precision, local standard scores should be used when at least 100 students in the age group are given the exact same test. In those instances where the group sizes are less than 100, the local standard score can be mathematically computed, but using the local raw score ranking is recommended.

Local Percentile Rank

Local percentile rank explains a student's performance relative to other students. These scores range from 1 to 99.9 and indicate the percentage of students who obtained the same or lower local standard score as the student. For example, if a student has a local percentile rank of 90, this indicates that they earned a raw score that was equal to or greater than 90 percent of students in the local norm sample.

To convert raw scores to a local percentile rank, it is necessary to use a cumulative frequency distribution for the local representative sample. Local and national percentile ranks are commonly used in education, but it is important to understand that these scores are not the same as the percent of correct answers. Additionally, they should not be used in any mathematical calculations, because differences in percentile ranks are not equivalent units of measurement. That is, the difference between the standard scores of 110, 120, and 130 is always ten points. However, the differences between the percentile scores that correspond to the standard scores 110 and 120 is 16, and 120 and 130 is 7. Percentile ranks are somewhat easier to understand than a standard score. Even so, only standard scores should be used when comparing scores obtained on different tests (for example, when comparing scores on the Naglieri-V, Naglieri-NV, and Naglieri-Q).

Stanine Scores

Some states require districts to use stanine scores, which can also be obtained using local norms. Stanine scores range from 1 to 9 and have an average value of 5. Local stanines can be computed using the local norm sample average score and standard deviation. Stanine scores are relatively easy to use because they are all one-digit numbers. The major advantage of stanines is that the broad groupings discourage overinterpretation of small, insignificant differences among test scores. Stanine scores between 4 and 6 are considered within the average range, while scores as low as 1 or as high as 9 occur more rarely and denote extremely low or high performance, respectively.

An Example of Local Norm Calculations

To provide an example of the local norming process, we have created an illustration involving 100 cases. We are using a small sample simply to show how a local norming process might work, not to suggest that local norming is typically conducted on such a scale. The small data set makes the discussion more workable.

We begin by describing the total sample graphically in **figure 4.2**. The graph shows the frequency of cases with various raw scores on an imaginary test. Examination of the frequency distribution (referred to as a bimodal distribution) indicates that there are two groups of students that have average raw scores around 24 and 38.

To explain how norming could be accomplished, we created the three sets of local norms presented in **figure 4.3**. The first group is based on all four third-grade classes in a district combined. The second group is based on classes 1 and 2, and the third group on classes 3 and 4. Why might an administrator need to understand the frequency distribution? Assume that a school district has four elementary schools, two each in very different parts of the community that differ in their demographics. Using local norms for each part of the community would ensure that scores more precisely describe students in relation to others of the same age, experience, and environment and represent the community within which students reside.

The three ways of computing local norms are provided in **figure 4.3**. The student identification number, raw score, rank, percentile, and standard scores based on the total sample of all four classes are in the leftmost section of the table. The middle and rightmost sections of the table each include two classes. Classes 1 and 2 are the group with an average score of 24, and classes 3 and 4 have an average score of 34. Those cases that achieved a local norm standard score of 120 and above are highlighted. Notice that student number 32 earned a raw score of 40, rank of 4, percentile of 95, and standard score of 125 based on the scores earned by all the students in the four classes. That same student earned a rank of 1, percentile of 99, and standard score of 135 when compared to the students in classes 1 and 2 only. Thus, the same raw score of 40 yields different ranks, percentiles, and standard scores as the reference group changes. This is what is expected.

FIGURE 4.2 Raw Score Frequency

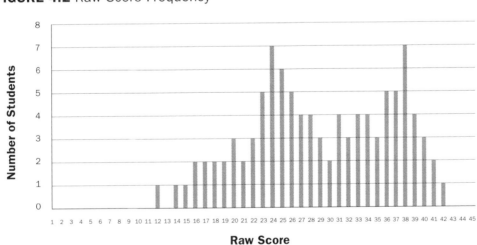

FIGURE 4.3 Local Norms Example

Student ID	Student Raw Score	Local Rank	Local Percentile	Standard Score		Student ID	Student Raw Score	Local Rank	Local Percentile	Standard Score		Student ID	Student Raw Score	Local Rank	Local Percentile	Standard Score
All Grade 3 Classes						**Grade 3 Classes 1 and 2**						**Grade 3 Classes 3 and 4**				
8	42	1	99	135		32	40	1	99	135		8	42	1	99	135
68	41	2	98	131		89	39	2	98	131		68	41	2	96	126
13	41	2	98	131		43	37	3	96	126		13	41	2	96	126
32	40	4	95	125		39	36	4	94	123		10	40	4	92	121
10	40	4	95	125		91	34	5	92	121		61	40	4	92	121
61	40	4	95	125		87	32	6	90	119		80	39	6	85	116
89	39	7	91	120		51	30	7	88	118		81	39	6	85	116
80	39	7	91	120		78	29	8	84	115		17	39	6	85	116
81	39	7	91	120		94	29	8	84	115		27	38	9	71	108
17	39	7	91	120		41	28	10	78	112		79	38	9	71	108
27	38	11	84	115		7	28	10	78	112		35	38	9	71	108
79	38	11	84	115		38	28	10	78	112		4	38	9	71	108
35	38	11	84	115		23	27	13	72	109		56	38	9	71	108
4	38	11	84	115		73	27	13	72	109		30	38	9	71	108
56	38	11	84	115		2	27	13	72	109		47	38	9	71	108
30	38	11	84	115		52	26	16	64	105		34	37	16	63	105
47	38	11	84	115		18	26	16	64	105		22	37	16	63	105
34	37	18	79	112		74	26	16	64	105		31	37	16	63	105
22	37	18	79	112		82	26	16	64	105		60	37	16	63	105
31	37	18	79	112		50	25	20	56	102		96	36	20	54	102
60	37	18	79	112		45	25	20	56	102		1	36	20	54	102
43	37	18	79	112		20	25	20	56	102		70	36	20	54	102
96	36	23	74	110		62	25	20	56	102		3	36	20	54	102
1	36	23	74	110		6	24	24	46	98		85	35	24	48	99
70	36	23	74	110		24	24	24	46	98		33	35	24	48	99

All Grade 3 Classes				
39	36	23	74	110
3	36	23	74	110
85	35	28	71	108
33	35	28	71	108
65	35	28	71	108
37	34	31	67	106
53	34	31	67	106
86	34	31	67	106
91	34	31	67	106
55	33	35	63	105
58	33	35	63	105
49	33	35	63	105
11	33	35	63	105
36	32	39	60	104
77	32	39	60	104
87	32	39	60	104
15	31	42	56	102
72	31	42	56	102
99	31	42	56	102
92	31	42	56	102

Grade 3 Classes 1 and 2				
84	24	24	46	98
75	24	24	46	98
98	24	24	46	98
63	23	29	38	95
88	23	29	38	95
95	23	29	38	95
44	23	29	38	95
57	22	33	32	93
19	22	33	32	93
42	22	33	32	93
5	21	36	28	91
54	21	36	28	91
9	20	38	22	88
71	20	38	22	88
26	20	38	22	88
76	19	41	18	86
48	19	41	18	86
12	18	43	14	84
90	18	43	14	84
21	17	45	10	81

Grade 3 Classes 3 and 4				
65	35	24	48	99
37	34	27	42	97
53	34	27	42	97
86	34	27	42	97
55	33	30	33	94
58	33	30	33	94
49	33	30	33	94
11	33	30	33	94
36	32	34	29	92
77	32	34	29	92
15	31	36	21	88
72	31	36	21	88
99	31	36	21	88
92	31	36	21	88
25	30	40	19	87
66	2	41	17	85
40	28	42	15	84
100	27	43	13	83
16	26	44	10	81
29	25	45	6	77

Values associated with raw scores less than 30 are omitted.

All Grade 3 Classes					Grade 3 Classes 1 and 2					Grade 3 Classes 3 and 4				
Mn	29	48.9	48.3	99	Mn	24.2	25.1	48.2	99.2	Mn	34	23.8	47.5	98.6
SD	7.4	29.2	29.1	15.1	SD	6.2	14.9	29.6	15.5	SD	5	14.7	28.9	15.2
N	100	100	100	100	N	51	51	51	51	N	49	49	49	49

Challenges with Using Local Norms

Using local norms for identifying gifted students can help a district better match their gifted population to the local population. Despite the advantages, there are some things to consider and plan for when using local norms. Most districts do not have student populations that match the national population. Local norms are, by definition, a reflection of the community in which a student resides, rather than the country as a whole. This means that the local standard score, for example, may be different from a national standard score. If a student moves from one community to another, their local standard score obtained in relation to the new community may be different. For this reason, if families move to a different state, district, or school and wish to enter the gifted program, their local standard score may not be accepted. If a family anticipates mobility, the district may be able to provide national norm scores to transfer to a new district. If these are unavailable, a student may need to be retested in the new district. Districts that use only local norms instead of national norms must be careful about the language they use to identify the student as gifted since entry criteria vary between schools and school districts.

Score Interpretation Scenarios

Next we describe three hypothetical scenarios to help readers understand the varying needs of students commonly found in schools. Our purpose here is to provide realistic profiles of students, along with possible educational outcomes to consider. When reading through these scenarios, ask yourself if you recognize these students. Have you seen students with similar profiles at your school or program? If so, what kinds of interventions were needed?

Scenario 1: Isabella

Isabella is a third-grade Latina English language learner student in a medium-sized urban school district. This district's demographics are more than 80 percent students of color, 100 percent economically disadvantaged students, and more than 25 percent English language learners. Isabella is a good student who earns A's on her report card. She enjoys spending time with her friends and going to school. Her teacher recommended her for gifted testing, saying that she always finishes her work correctly and on time and is a leader in the classroom.

Isabella is highly successful and challenged in school. She is in the top-achieving group in her class, is well-adjusted socially and emotionally, and thrives learning with same-age peers. Isabella's test scores (see **figure 4.4**) indicate that her needs are not significantly different from those of the local norm group. Therefore, her needs can be met in the regular classroom with occasional curricular modifications when needed.

FIGURE 4.4: Isabella's School Data

Achievement Test Scores	
Language Arts	119 standard score; 90th percentile
Math	114 standard score; 83rd percentile
Naglieri General Ability Tests Scores	
Verbal	110 standard score; 74th percentile
Nonverbal	102 standard score; 55th percentile
Quantitative	100 standard score; 50th percentile
SES Status	Qualifies for free lunch
SPED Needs	No IEP or 504
Decision	No special services needed

Scenario 2: Angel

Angel is a fifth-grade Black student in a large urban school district. As a result of his family living in poverty, which among other things hampers their ability to cover basic costs of living, he qualifies for free breakfast and lunch. The district he attends has more than 60 percent students of color, more than 65 percent economically disadvantaged students, and more than 11 percent English language learners. Angel earns A's in subjects he enjoys but struggles in classes that don't interest him. He has a few close friends who share his interests. Angel was not recommended for testing by his teachers, but he participated in universal testing for all fifth graders in the district. Angel's scores are detailed in **figure 4.5**.

FIGURE 4.5 Angel's School Data

Achievement Test Scores	
Language Arts	110 standard score; 74th percentile
Math	136 standard score; 99th percentile
Naglieri General Ability Tests Scores	
Verbal	120 standard score; 92nd percentile
Nonverbal	130 standard score; 98th percentile

Quantitative	135 standard score; 99th percentile
SES Status	Qualifies for free breakfast and lunch
SPED Needs	No IEP or 504
Decision	Special services needed

Angel is a really smart kid. His test scores indicate that his needs are significantly different from those of the local norm group and, therefore, cannot be met in the regular classroom. Angel needs specialized services at school and support at home. For his social and emotional development, he needs time to be with other gifted students in a variety of settings. The best solution for this is cluster grouping* within his grade level.

In addition to cluster grouping, Angel should be considered for acceleration. The first step in this process would be to administer an end-of-year math assessment to determine his mathematical skill level. If he scores an 85 percent or higher, he should be placed in the next level of math. It will be important for Angel to be part of this decision and supported by both his current fifth-grade teacher and the higher-level math teacher. Schedules will need to be coordinated and support will need to be available to Angel as he adjusts to a new math level.

Angel will also benefit from enrichment opportunities in his areas of interest. An interview with Angel can help determine clubs, competitions, and activities that interest him. Possibilities include robotics, e-sports, or math competitions. It is important to note that due to his poverty status, home support needs to be well thought out and enrichment services should not financially burden the family. If there are fees associated with clubs or competitions, these need to be covered by the school or an outside group. (In Arizona, the state gifted association has funding for students in need. Check with your state gifted association for help.)

Angel's parents need to understand his test scores, what his learning needs are, and how his needs can be met at school and at home. This can be done in a face-to-face meeting, in a video meeting, or on a phone call. Due to cultural norms, some parents may resist calling attention to their child and will not allow their child to receive specialized services. In addition, there is a possibility that, due to the family's low socioeconomic status, Angel's parents may resist any added school obligations, especially if funds are required. The parents need time to receive information, ask questions, and feel supported. Since Angel goes to a large school district, this support may be limited. If so, a parent representative may be available to share general information about gifted services.

Angel's teachers also need to understand his test scores, what his learning needs are, and how to meet his needs at school. Learning about gifted students

*The schoolwide cluster grouping model (SCGM) is a method for providing full-time gifted education services without major budget implications, and with potential to raise achievement for all students. With the SCGM, all students are purposefully placed into classrooms based on their abilities, potential, or achievement. A group of gifted-identified students is clustered into a mixed-ability classroom with a teacher who is trained to differentiate for gifted students (Winebrenner and Brulles 2018).

through professional development in person, online, or through gifted education resource guides is highly recommended.

Scenario 3: Alex

Alex is a White kindergartener in a rural school district. Most of the families, including Alex's, are farmers and agricultural workers who work very long hours or may work more than one job to make ends meet. The district has fewer than 600 students, with only one elementary school, one middle school, and one high school. This district's demographics are more than 15 percent students of color, more than 85 percent economically disadvantaged students, and more than 50 percent English language learners. Students living in these conditions usually have limited learning opportunities outside of school and are less likely to be identified as gifted.

Regardless, Alex taught himself to read at three and is reading chapter books in kindergarten. His mother describes him as having a thirst for knowledge. Alex gets very frustrated by the pace of learning in his kindergarten class and refuses to do the work that the teacher assigns. Alex has unique characteristics, including intense interests in black holes and Harry Potter that are not commonly shared by other kindergartners, resulting in social isolation and emotional outbursts at school. Fortunately, the district provides universal screening and Alex was identified as having special needs. Alex's test scores are shown in **figure 4.6.**

FIGURE 4.6 Alex's School Data

Achievement Test Scores	
Language Arts	136 standard score; 99th percentile
Math	136 standard score; 99th percentile
Naglieri General Ability Tests Scores	
Verbal	132 standard score; 98th percentile
Nonverbal	136 standard score; 99th percentile
Quantitative	130 standard score; 98th percentile
SES Status	Qualifies for reduced lunch
SPED Needs	504 for social and emotional support
Decision	Special services needed

Alex is a really smart kid who needs specialized services to meet his academic, social, and emotional needs. Alex's test scores indicate that his needs are significantly different from those of the local norm group. Therefore, his needs cannot be met in the regular classroom.

Alex will benefit from specialized services at his school. Since he is significantly advanced compared to the group being tested, he should be considered for acceleration, in either a single subject or a whole grade level. There are several things to consider with both these options.

First, it is important for the team making this decision, which includes Alex and his parents, to understand the positive aspects and the challenges associated with whole-grade-level acceleration. They should review the research from the Belin-Blank Center for gifted education and talent development (belinblank. education.uiowa.edu).

To make this important decision, Alex's parents need to understand his test scores, his learning needs, and how his needs can be met at school and at home. This can be done in a face-to-face meeting, in a video meeting, or on a phone call. Alex's parents need time to receive information, ask questions, and feel supported. Since Alex's family works long hours and has limited resources, there is a possibility that his parents may resist any added school obligations, especially if funds are required. It will be important to provide resources for Alex to have at home in addition to resources at school.

Alex has a 504 plan for social and emotional needs. A 504 plan is an accommodation plan to ensure that a student who has a disability receives accommodations to ensure their academic success. Since Alex goes to a small school district, the 504 plan can be supported by the principal, school counselor, and special education teacher. This plan should include strategies to help Alex learn how to make friends and support his developing social skills.

Alex's teachers need to understand his test scores, his learning needs, and how his needs can be met at school. We highly recommend professional development in person, online, or through gifted education resource guides.

Next Steps

Once students like Angel and Alex are identified for gifted services, what happens next? After a gifted student is identified based on their ability to think clearly and deeply, then educators can work toward ensuring they provide curricula to meet the student's academic needs. In essence, this means that school administrators need to establish a system wherein the curriculum and instruction support and develop students' advanced learning needs. However, far too often we see the reverse scenario: school administrators seeking to identify students who will do well in existing gifted programs often overlook students with high ability whose learning needs differ from the programs or services offered. In chapter 5, we describe ways that school administrators can build comprehensive services that address the academic needs of all students with high ability (even those who are not yet highly achieving). And we share ways to modify existing programs and services.

Modifying gifted services to accommodate students' learning needs after using local norms seems a logical assumption. Keep in mind that using local norms will likely shift the composition of the gifted program to better reflect the demographics of the community. The newly identified students may not have fit the previous qualifying criteria for, and/or purpose of, the existing program. This means that the methods used to serve gifted students will need to change to be more inclusive of newly identified students who have been historically underrepresented in gifted programs.

Chapter Summary

This chapter discussed and presented ideas for what to do after students are tested. We offered a variety of ways to consider and use test scores and explained the importance of communicating with parents and teachers. We presented methods for using local and national norms and offered suggestions for implementing them. Suggestions for gifted programming structures and modifications are discussed in detail in part 3.

PART THREE
Instructional Approaches

5
The Next Step: Achieving Equity in Gifted Programming

School administrators of gifted programs struggle in their efforts to make gifted education more inclusive. While most school districts clearly recognize and acknowledge that their schools do not effectively identify and serve gifted students in certain populations or subgroups, few do enough to rectify this discrepancy. To achieve equity, schools must expand their views, procedures, and practices on the gifted identification process while providing tiered levels of services and instructional support based on students' needs (Peters and Brulles 2017). School personnel must broaden and expand gifted identification and services to be more responsive to students who have previously been disenfranchised. This begins with inclusive practices for identifying giftedness. Once previously missing students are identified, the questions become:

➤ How do we serve our diverse gifted population?

➤ What do we do if these newly identified gifted students are not demonstrating the high levels of achievement that are needed for success in gifted programs?

➤ How can we determine if students are engaging in the gifted services being offered? What can we change when students do not actively engage?

➤ How can we better structure our gifted programs in ways that are diverse, equitable, and inclusive?

Thus far, we have focused on identification tools and processes that embrace diversity and equity. But improving these procedures is only the first step toward achieving equity in gifted programs. Chapters 5 and 6 explore methods for developing inclusive practices that enfranchise, respect, and champion high-ability learners who have previously been denied or limited in their access to gifted education opportunities at school.

In this chapter, we challenge readers to reassess their current practices and procedures. We ask, *What is your ultimate goal when considering the current state of your gifted programs or services?* We encourage school and district teams—including school administrators, gifted coordinators, and teachers—to reflect on the following questions when considering the *who*, *what*, and *how* in building equitable programs:

➤ What actions can you take to increase diversity, equity, and inclusion in your program?

➤ What do you need to know to undertake these actions?

➤ What approach(es) do you want to use?

➤ Who should be involved in the process?

To answer these questions, you likely need to transition away from past practices and focus instead on changes to transform your services. This involves examining what barriers exist and considering how to go about solving the problem.

In earlier chapters, we identified historical obstacles to equity in gifted identification. We reported that there are more than one million students from low socioeconomic status and non-White populations who are missing from gifted education. With this large a number of unidentified and underserved gifted students, it is important to ask why schools are missing these students. Is it due solely to an inability to identify them? Or are the gifted services and programs themselves serving as barriers to diverse learners of high ability? Identifying and understanding failures in practice leads directly to ideas for action. An action-oriented process requires that educators, schools, and districts also examine how personal culture, biases, and beliefs influence their efforts in providing gifted services.

To make necessary progress, schools and districts need to identify the patterns, beliefs, and assumptions that are the foundation of their current programs and services. Only after identifying these obstacles can services be rebuilt upon an ability-based approach to achieve the goal of equity in gifted education. In this chapter, we focus on what needs to change in gifted programming. These changes rely primarily on shifting mindsets, building relationships, and examining your purpose and approaches in serving gifted learners.

Glossary of Terms for Diversity as Related to Gifted Programming

The terms defined here provide context to the topics discussed and explored throughout chapters 5 and 6, as pertaining to the provision of gifted services and programming.

Term	Definition
Bias	A personal and unjustifiable judgment or prejudice that favors or goes against an individual, a group, or a belief. Bias can also be seen in gifted identification tools that prohibit some groups of students from participating in gifted services.

Continuum of services	A range of gifted services designed to be inclusive of varied levels of giftedness.
Culturally responsive pedagogy	A student-centered instructional approach that aligns with and nurtures students' unique cultural strengths to promote academic achievement while supporting and developing emotional well-being.
Culturally responsive teaching	Working toward equity by examining one's own biases and by being willing to listen to students, and then modifying instruction to respond purposefully and effectively.
Disproportionality	Disparities in student populations of gifted education programs commonly stemming from inequities in gifted identification.
Equity	All students have an equal opportunity to demonstrate their ability to think and learn. This means ensuring that everyone receives what they need to be successful and recognizing that these needs vary across racial, cultural, and socioeconomic lines. Equity in gifted education focuses on identifying and serving a diverse population representative of the student body at large.
Inclusion	Putting diversity into action by developing and supporting gifted programs that involve, honor, and respect students with diverse backgrounds and perspectives.
Inclusionary services	Proactively and purposefully enfranchise students representative of the school's or district's student populations.
Mindsets	The established set of attitudes people hold that lead to cultural bias, racism, and classism; interfere with diversity in thought; and inhibit actions that lead to equity. Mindsets contribute to underrepresentation in gifted programs, but when enlightened, mindsets can lead to changes in practices.
Racism	The belief that people of some races are inferior to others, and the thoughts, actions, and policies that result from this belief. Racist behaviors are demonstrated as prejudice, discrimination, and aggression against some and unfair advantages to others. Underrepresentation in gifted education is a result of racism in the field.

Talent development	Deliberately providing opportunities for students to pursue areas of strength and explore interests by engaging in enriching activities to develop potential. Talent development is inclusive of academics, athletics, and visual and performing arts.
Underrepresentation	When students from marginalized groups are not identified as gifted and therefore are not appropriately represented in gifted programs.
Underserved populations	Student populations commonly missing from or not engaging in gifted programs due to underidentification or to not feeling welcomed or appreciated in the structure of the services offered.

Providing Context: Background, Current Circumstances, and Moving Forward

Chapter 1 provided a brief history of ability testing and highlighted the reasons and need for new approaches in gifted identification procedures. Consider that entrance into many gifted programs requires scoring highly on a nationally normed ability test. The move to using local norms, and especially building norms, means that schools and districts must alter their gifted program entrance criteria. In this context, schools likely need to modify or redesign their gifted programming and services.

Reasons for a redesign when using local norms vary depending on the school's or district's existing programs. For example, newly identified students may not meet preexisting entrance criteria when the program or service model requires both high ability and high achievement or if the services favor subject acceleration. Another example of a service model that may need to be redesigned is when the district buses gifted students to a central school site. Families from some cultures prefer to have siblings remain at the same school rather than one child attending a separate site for gifted services. And some simply do not want their children singled out for "different" services. Various gifted program models and their barriers to equity, as well as possible solutions, are discussed in more detail later in this chapter.

Decades of expert research in the field have greatly increased attention and efforts to reverse injustices that have served as barriers to participation for many gifted learners of color, English language learners, and students living in poverty. Despite this increased attention, underrepresentation of these populations continues, in large part because of program entrance criteria. The current movement toward using universal testing and local norms in gifted identification shows tremendous potential for fulfilling those efforts, if the data is sufficiently valued. The logic used when aggregating data about a student can aid or hinder identification, thereby either supporting inclusive gifted programming or limiting access to some students with high ability. In other words, data can help schools determine the most appropriate cutoff scores to use. This data then influences program entrance criteria and the students the school identifies as needing beyond-grade-level instruction.

Shifting Mindsets and Perspectives

Inequities in gifted education programs reflect systemic failures (Ecker-Lyster and Niileksela 2017; Hodges, McIntosh, and Gentry 2017). For example, Sullivan (2011) found that socioeconomic status (SES) and race are the best predictors for placement into a gifted program. Students from low SES backgrounds are placed at a lower rate than students from high SES backgrounds, and Latino and Black students are placed at a lower rate than White and Asian students (Hodges, McIntosh, and Gentry 2017, 206). These failures are due to the longstanding and biased systems schools have held in place that favor certain student populations over others. These failed systems are now under great scrutiny and are drawing national attention (Ford et al. 2018).

The shift toward more progressive and just practices needs to happen across all areas of gifted services. With evolving identification processes that seek to broaden the makeup of gifted populations, such as universal testing and the use of local norms, schools have the opportunity to support students who have previously been kept out of gifted programs. Educators are now considering how to change systems and mindsets that have long prevented such progress.

Ensuring equity in gifted education requires educators, schools, and districts to develop cultural awareness and cultural competency. This shift in cultural perspective allows schools to outline new identification processes and criteria that do not rely on characteristics of those historically served in gifted programs: predominantly White, native-English-speaking, middle- and upper-middle-class students. By examining previously held mindsets and increasing cultural awareness and competency, educators can become better able to see all gifted learners.

To rebuild gifted services in more equitable ways that promote diversity, stakeholders must consider and acknowledge their personal roles in perpetuating these unacceptable yet entrenched practices. Rebuilding gifted services starts with awareness of how school policies can add to, and even set the stage for, the overrepresentation of White, affluent students—and corresponding underrepresentation of Black, Hispanic, and Native

> Rebuilding gifted services starts with awareness of how school policies can add to, and even set the stage for, the overrepresentation of White, affluent students—and corresponding underrepresentation of Black, Hispanic, and Native American students; English language learners; and students living in poverty—in gifted programming.

American students; English language learners; and students living in poverty—in gifted programming. Mindsets impact policies, so examining existing policies in light of changing mindsets should be a priority and a prerequisite when redesigning gifted programs.

Redesigning Gifted Education Policies

Educators and administrators must ask themselves which policies and procedures are contributing to underrepresentation. Ford (2014) emphasizes that "educators, decision makers, and policy makers must analyze and eliminate intentional and unintentional discriminatory barriers to gifted education, as such roadblocks have the same impact or outcomes—underrepresentation and segregation" (148–149). Policies to consider evaluating include reliance on teacher referral or checklists versus schoolwide grade-level screening, parent/caregiver referral or checklists, designated cutoff scores, the grades at which gifted programs begin, whether screening is ongoing, convenience and location of testing sites, communication methods, and more.

It is not enough for educators and administrators to examine just their policies. They must go further.

It is not enough for educators and administrators to examine just their policies. They must go further and examine the intended and unintended outcomes of those policies. In *A Culturally Responsive Equity-Based Bill of Rights for Gifted Students of Color*, Ford and colleagues state: "Educators might ask these questions: (a) How do policies and procedures and assessments contribute to underrepresentation? (b) When was the last time the district's gifted program and services were evaluated by an external and culturally competent program evaluator(s) with gifted education expertise? And (c) In what ways can the features and components of my program better reflect items in the Equity-Based Bill of Rights for Gifted Students of Color?" (Ford et al. 2018, 126).

The Equity-Based Bill of Rights for Gifted Students of Color was developed by Ford and other gifted experts to help practitioners, administrators, families, and communities understand the needs of gifted students of color and to address the specific needs of underrepresented populations. The authors state, "This Bill of Rights was envisioned with the singular goal of effecting change based on equity and cultural responsiveness. Our rationale is that gifted students of color have rights that must be heard, honored, and addressed. They have gifts and talents that must be recognized, affirmed, and developed as districts endeavor to recruit and retain them in gifted education" (Ford et al. 2018, 125).

The tenets presented in *A Culturally Responsive Equity-Based Bill of Rights for Gifted Students of Color* challenge educators and administrators to analyze data for underrepresentation and attitudes (deficit thinking) so that inequitable practices become acknowledged, examined, analyzed, challenged, and corrected.

The Equity-Based Bill of Rights for Gifted Students of Color asks the following questions of educators (Ford 2018, 150):

➤ "Are Hispanic and African American students being screened in proportion to their representation in the district?"

➤ "What is the magnitude or severity of underrepresentation?"

➤ "What are the contributing factors to underrepresentation (and under-referral), such as attitudes and values, instruments, and policies and procedures?"

➤ "Which teachers/educators under-refer culturally diverse groups? How are they being assisted and held accountable?"

➤ "Which policies and procedures are contributing to underrepresentation (e.g., reliance on teacher referral or checklists versus schoolwide grade-level screening, parent/caregiver referral or checklists, designated cutoff scores, grade at which gifted programs begin, whether screening is ongoing, convenience and location of testing sites, methods of communicating with the community, and more)?"

➤ "How would underrepresentation decrease if teacher referrals were eliminated and if different instruments were adopted?"

➤ "How does other information collected contribute to underrepresentation (e.g., grades, products, parent/caregiver forms)?"

This list provides specific questions schools should ask to help frame and direct their efforts. Recognizing and acknowledging areas of need represents a tremendous leap toward correcting injustices and overcoming obstacles that have sustained underrepresentation of specific populations. These questions are critical in focusing schools' efforts when reframing gifted services.

High General Ability Without High Achievement: Another Shift in Perspective

In chapter 3, we described how a student's "level" of giftedness impacts the degree of curriculum modification they need. It is important to note that no assumption should be made as to *which* gifted students fall into which levels of giftedness. For example, a student who is learning English may score at the 99th percentile on all three Naglieri General Ability Tests. These scores indicate that the student is able to acquire information at a very high level, regardless of their English language proficiency. This means their gifted program placement and instruction would be at the very highest level, even if they are not fluent in English. A native-English-speaking student may earn percentile scores of 62, 97, and 64 on the verbal, quantitative, and nonverbal tests, respectively. This second student likely falls into the bright or gifted level and would therefore not likely need the same level of modification to instruction as would the first student.

Regardless of their level of giftedness, students of color, English language learners, and students living in poverty are more likely to be left out of gifted services (Gentry et al. 2019). This disparity is especially evident when school systems require students identified as having high ability to also demonstrate advanced academic achievement. These students, who have demonstrated high ability but who are not yet highly achieving, may have lacked similar opportunities to learn as their White or more affluent peers. By including them in gifted services, we give them access to learning experiences that will help them develop their areas of academic strength.

No assumption should be made as to *which* gifted students fall into which levels of giftedness.

Some fear that schools will diminish the rigor of their gifted services by not requiring students to demonstrate a certain level of academic achievement. This fear can be mitigated by developing a continuum of services and supports within the gifted program, instead of using a rigid one-size-fits-all approach.

Gifted learners are not a homogeneous group. They do not all share similar learning experiences based on their racial, ethnic, or cultural backgrounds and perspectives; prior learning experiences; academic achievement; and opportunity gaps. Even so, they all share high general ability. This means that teachers of gifted learners should emphasize a strengths-based approach to instruction. This approach is important in any setting in which gifted students are placed and will be expanded upon in chapter 6.

Obstacles and Solutions for English Language Learners

The barriers to identification discussed in chapter 1 are not the only obstacles gifted English language learners encounter. In an article published in *EdWeek* on October 26, 2020, Larry Ferlazzo described several mistakes educators make when teaching students who are learning English. Two of those "mistakes," as they relate to equity in gifted education, include "confusing lack of proficiency in English with lack of intelligence" and "looking at [English language learners] through the lens of deficits instead of assets."

The first mistake involves the problem created when acceptance into a gifted program also requires a certain level of achievement. This practice excludes many English language learners from gifted education, since they may be unable to demonstrate high achievement due to a lack of English language proficiency. This is one area where schools can rethink their gifted program entrance criteria. Once it is established that English language learners have high general ability, as measured on the Naglieri General Ability Tests, excluding them from gifted services based on lack of English proficiency ignores their demonstrated high ability and is an injustice to this group of gifted learners. Olszewski-Kubilius and Clarenbach write that as our nation becomes increasingly more diverse, the educational system is tasked with the responsibility of developing high levels of talent among all groups of children by providing equitable education (2014). This ambitious task includes our growing population of students learning English and all students from underserved groups in gifted education.

The second mistake Ferlazzo shared is that schools too often view English language learners through a deficit lens rather than acknowledging their strengths. Navigating through two languages stimulates thought, provides multiple perspectives, and requires reflection, all of which enhance learning and critical thinking. These abilities are assets that we need to encourage in our gifted learners, not disparage!

Gifted Programming Approaches for Serving Underrepresented Populations

A question that schools and districts throughout the United States wrestle with is how to achieve equity in ways that ensure all students can fully access academic, social, and emotional supports and appropriate services. Some schools and districts asking this question will find that they need to transition away from past practices and rethink their ideas about what is needed. An agreed-upon premise to begin considering change might simply be that giftedness runs across all cultures,

What areas of programming need to be reassessed?

races, and ethnicities, as well as genders, socioeconomic statuses, and English language proficiency levels (NAGC 2021). With that in mind, schools should expect and strive to identify and serve all gifted learners, and especially those who have been previously underserved. Once they reframe their vision in this way, schools can then ask the action-oriented question: *What areas of programming need to be reassessed?*

Ford wrote that creating equitable services requires a deep dive into our student data and forewarns that this is an all-encompassing process. She states, "Districts must be diligent about studying, evaluating, and disaggregating their student demographics (taking into account race, income, gender, and language) and proactively and aggressively advocating for underrepresented students from such groups" (2014, 145). Only after examining the current status of their gifted programs using measurable data can schools begin to identify the steps they need to take in this direction.

Remember that equity means that all students receive the support they need, whatever that support may be. This requires that schools and districts personalize both gifted service design and instruction for the students actually in their buildings and programs. To be inclusive and culturally responsive, gifted programming needs to move away from a one-size-fits-all approach and focus attention on developing each student's personal potential.

With this in mind, educators must consider the discrepancy in students' access to opportunities outside of school when designing gifted programs. Ensuring that gifted services provide equal access to a wide range of gifted learners and scaffold learning for students requires developing a continuum of services. When a continuum of services is not feasible, as in small or rural districts, then a continuum of instructional approaches can appropriately serve a diverse range of gifted learners. (This type of instructional approach is discussed further in chapter 6.)

Given the organic nature of using local norms for gifted identification (see chapter 4) and access to services, there is no such thing as an "ideal" approach to serving a diverse group of gifted learners. Schools must design services based on the students they have identified. Regardless of the structure developed, some imperative features exist when designing gifted services for a diverse group of students, including flexible and cluster grouping and language support in every gifted classroom with an English language learner.

Cluster Grouping and Flexible Grouping

Research shows there is approximately a seven- to eight-grade-level span of achievement in any given classroom (Peters et al. 2020; Peters 2017). **Figures 5.1** and **5.2** visually represent how broad the learning levels can be and portray the critical need to group students for instruction. Teachers cannot assume that all students benefit from grade-level instruction, nor can they assume that all gifted students should be accelerated in all content areas. Remember, equity in education means ensuring that everyone receives what they need in order to learn.

FIGURE 5.1 Reading Levels of Students in a Fourth-Grade Classroom

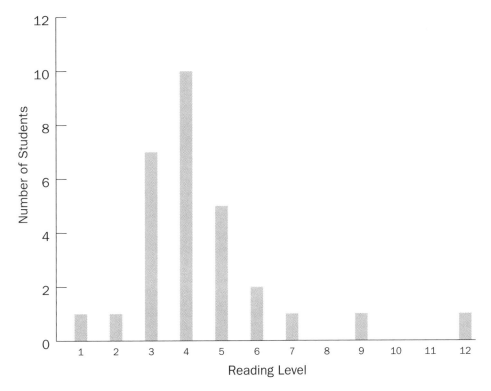

Copyright © NWEA. Used with permission.

FIGURE 5.2 Instructional Levels Needed in a Fifth-Grade Classroom

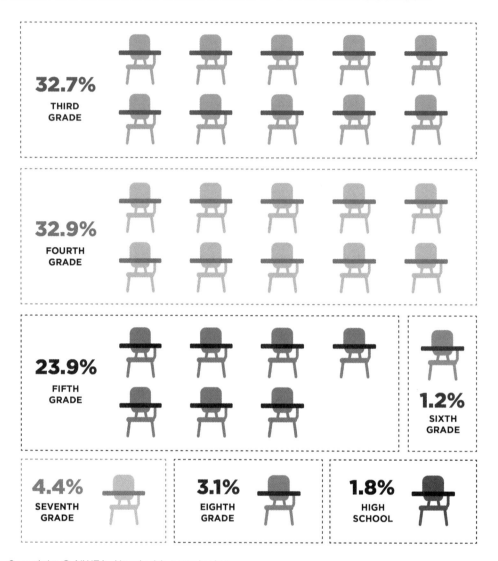

32.7% THIRD GRADE	
32.9% FOURTH GRADE	
23.9% FIFTH GRADE	**1.2%** SIXTH GRADE
4.4% SEVENTH GRADE	**3.1%** EIGHTH GRADE
	1.8% HIGH SCHOOL

Despite the best intentions, and even with extensive training, the wide range of abilities present in a single classroom can prevent teachers from providing equitable instruction. However, by grouping students based on their learning needs, teachers can accomplish this challenging task. This is especially true in the elementary grades when one teacher is typically responsible for teaching all content areas. Cluster grouping allows this to occur throughout an entire grade level, while flexible grouping can serve the same purpose within a classroom.

Cluster grouping and flexible grouping are two important grouping methods that can powerfully impact learning for all gifted students. In a cluster grouping model, gifted students are grouped together in one classroom at each grade level. Ideally in this model, the range of abilities in each classroom has been narrowed so that none of the teachers in a grade level has students on both ends of the instructional spectrum. For example, students who need below-grade-level modifications and instruction would not be placed in the same classroom as the gifted cluster students. This slightly narrowed range of ability levels in the class assists the teacher in designing lessons and carrying out instruction at appropriate levels (Brulles, Saunders, and Cohn 2010).

A main benefit for gifted students in a gifted cluster class is that they have like-minded peers with whom they can learn on a daily basis. Many students newly identified on the Naglieri General Ability Tests will also be grouped with peers from their cultural groups. This occurs when using building norms because more culturally and linguistically diverse students will be identified overall. When grouped together for all their content areas, gifted students are more likely to challenge themselves, delve deeper into the content, and engage in critical and creative thinking. Grouping gifted learners together also gives them comfort in knowing that there are others who may feel and view things the way they do (Brulles and Winebrenner 2019). Similarly, gifted students feel more comfortable and accepted when grouped with other gifted students from similar cultural groups. This camaraderie promotes a feeling of acceptance, and with this, students are more likely to pursue academic challenges that further their learning possibilities. *The Cluster Grouping Handbook* by Dina Brulles and Susan Winebrenner (2019) provides extensive guidance on how to structure, implement, and teach in the cluster grouping model.

Flexible grouping practices take many forms: they can occur informally within a classroom, throughout a grade level, or even between grade levels. In *A Teacher's Guide to Flexible Grouping and Collaborative Learning*, Dina Brulles and Karen Brown (2018) describe two main variations of flexible grouping: regrouping for specific instruction and within-class groupings. They describe how flexible grouping enables continual assessment, targeted instruction, focus on specific learning objectives, learner confidence, and differentiated instruction.

> A main benefit for gifted students in a gifted cluster class is that they have like-minded peers with whom they can learn on a daily basis.

Flexible grouping practices can occur in any classroom, whether that be a self-contained gifted class, a gifted cluster class, or a general education class. Flexible groups are just that . . . flexible! This means that students are grouped and regrouped depending on the lesson. Teachers can form flexible groups of students within a class by ability, interests, performance, readiness, preference, and/or learning objectives. Having multiple ways to form flexible groups is critical when serving a range of gifted learners because it respects that students will be at varied learning levels within the content being taught. It also allows students to work in ways they feel most comfortable, pursue interests, build on strengths, and work at their personal readiness levels within the content (Brulles and Brown 2018).

Regardless of the method employed, gifted learners will benefit from these grouping practices by having opportunities to work at their levels of readiness and develop their interests. As an example, consider a group of Hispanic English language learners who are identified as having a need for gifted services in a grade level where all students were screened using the Naglieri General Ability

Tests. This scenario would be expected in a Title I school in an area with a high percentage of Hispanic and English language learner students. Using building norms as described in chapter 4, a certain percentage of that population would be identified as having a need for gifted services at that school. Grouping these students together, along with the other gifted students in the grade level, would give them both intellectual and cultural peers, which greatly enhances student engagement, collaboration, and sense of belonging. Teachers will see the need to learn more culturally responsive methods to support these newly identified students.

Language Support for Gifted English Language Learners

Most states have mandates that describe structures and guidelines for supporting English language learners. In many states, placement into ELL classes is mandatory until students reach specific levels of English proficiency. However, there is a significant number of English language learners who are also gifted, whether or not they are yet identified as such. The number of students in a school with a dual identity of ELL and gifted can be expected to increase when using the Naglieri General Ability Tests with building norms and appropriate weighting of the findings. As schools identify these students, they must also ensure that their gifted programs address the students' unique learning needs—as both English language learners and gifted learners.

Schools can take a couple of approaches in providing language support for gifted English language learners. One method is for the students to be clustered together with a gifted cluster teacher who is also an ELL teacher. Another is for the students to be placed in a gifted class with push-in or pull-out language support. In either of these approaches, it is important that teachers have training in both language acquisition and gifted education instruction.

Providing training in gifted education to language acquisition testers and all ELL teachers prepares them to recognize the signs of giftedness in English language learners. Regardless of the approach for providing language support, the placement, or the program, it is imperative that, once identified, gifted English language learners be included in the gifted program at the school site. Grouping with language support helps enfranchise these learners.

Characteristics of Gifted English Language Learners

- rapid acquisition of English language proficiency
- display of leadership within the student's cultural group
- extensive use of language within the student's primary language
- demonstration of inquisitiveness, curiosity, creativity, problem-solving, and drive for learning
- ease in transitioning between languages spoken

- innate abilities to see relationships between ideas, concepts, and information in general

- ability to generate original ideas

- signs of maturity, sensitivity, and insight

Using Local or Building Norms in Your Gifted Program

Once students have been identified using local norms, districts must then differentiate their gifted services based on the gifted student population. Having different identification and programming criteria for each school in a district is being culturally responsive. In this way, services become organic and develop based on need. Expect that by using the Naglieri General Ability Tests and building norms, you will need to prepare for different tiers of services.

This new approach likely involves considerable changes in how a school structures its gifted services. And there are a number of factors schools must take into account once they have an expanded and diverse pool of gifted students. It is critically important to consider not only how these newly identified students access instruction, but also how educators can support students' identities and attitudes in gifted programs. (See chapter 6 for a more detailed description of the support teachers can provide in the classroom.)

Developing a Strengths-Based Approach

We have discussed how using the Naglieri General Ability Tests along with local norms is a proactive, strengths-based approach to gifted identification that does not rely on evidence of high achievement or on school-based knowledge. In chapter 6, we will discuss how a strengths-based approach fits within instruction. But first, we must consider how such an approach comes into play with gifted programming, especially once new populations of gifted students are identified within a school or district.

> An evolution of services requires that educators focus on students' high ability and place them in programs that help them learn and grow.

Mindsets can create barriers to equity in gifted programming, which can become systemic obstacles to participation for some gifted students. Identifying the barriers inherent in some gifted programming models can guide school administrators to expand their vision and create more inclusive practices. Earlier in this chapter we cautioned that gifted programs are sometimes part of the problem and exacerbate underrepresentation. School administrators can address this by prioritizing students' high ability once they have identified the obstacles in their program model.

This evolution of services requires that educators focus on students' high ability and place them in programs that help them learn and grow. Education often works from a deficit model, with the goal of fixing what is an impediment. In this case, that means requiring students with high ability to also demonstrate high academic performance before being placed in gifted education. This requirement ignores students' potential and prohibits them from participating in an education system that addresses who they are as learners in their entirety. That said, we should be careful not to ignore the areas in which students need additional support, such as with gifted English language learners or twice-exceptional students.

In **figure 5.3** we list the most common gifted program models and discuss the inherent barriers they are likely to pose for high-ability students from underrepresented populations. We then suggest ways to overcome these obstacles to program access. This description can help guide schools in modifying existing programs, and it introduces new approaches to serving underrepresented gifted students.

FIGURE 5.3 Considerations for Equity in Gifted Programming Models

Programming Model	Possible Barriers to Equity	Suggested Solutions
Self-contained gifted (SCG)	When placement requires evidence of high achievement Using a one-size-fits-all instructional approach within the self-contained class	Also have a cluster grouping model in the school if the self-contained class is restrictive academically to some gifted students. Create a SCG program based solely on high ability, without a requirement for high achievement.
Honors classes	When participation requires demonstration of high achievement When instruction is predominantly based on acceleration	When serving gifted students through honors classes, also have a cluster grouping model if the honors program is restrictive academically to some groups. Create an honors program that includes students who demonstrate high ability, regardless of their achievement levels.
Itinerant/enrichment	When students are removed from a homeroom class for services When students must be bused to a different school for services	Include enrichment classes at each school site and at each grade level in the school, rather than busing students to a different school.

Programming Model	Possible Barriers to Equity	Suggested Solutions
Cluster grouping/ flexible grouping	When grouping models are confused with tracking When groups are formed solely by achievement levels	Make sure that all students who demonstrate high ability are included in gifted cluster classes regardless of the students' levels of achievement.

A Call to Action

The work of Dr. Donna Ford inspires us to help schools determine and address root causes of disproportionality in their gifted programs. To do this, educators can use surveys, interviews, focus groups, and case studies from culturally diverse students and caregivers regarding their experiences (Ford 2014, 150). We advise schools to:

◆ collect data on the experiences of gifted students of color and gifted English language learners.

  ▶ What are the experiences of your former and current students in gifted education?

◆ disaggregate data for the groups by gender and income

  ▶ What are the experiences of your students by gender? By socioeconomic status?

Collaborating with District Departments

Ensuring equity in gifted programs requires a systems approach. School administrators must thoroughly study and determine how existing structures perpetuate underrepresentation. Then they must identify what specific structures, such as administrative initiatives and district priorities, could provide access, support, and resources to underserved students.

Proactively building gifted services that are designed to enfranchise underrepresented populations begins by building stakeholder support. Stakeholders include district administrators, principals, teachers, and parents. They need to be aware of gifted students' specific needs, and also the limitations and inequities for underserved populations that are inherent in the existing structure. When advocating for stakeholder support, providing information to all groups associated with the school district is crucial for building sustainable services.

Gifted education services in most schools and school districts typically receive very little funding compared to other departments or areas, such as special education, language acquisition, and curriculum. Collaboration with the departments or administrators overseeing these areas helps build connections and support by accessing their resources and building a shared vision and infrastructure. This collaboration can assist in establishing equitable and sustainable gifted education services throughout the school system.

In this section, we outline recommendations for developing these relationships and creating specific strategies to devise new services, opportunities, and instruction for these learners. Consider collaborating with community education, human resources, curriculum development, professional learning, special education, language acquisition, grants, equity specialists, principal groups, school psychologists, school counselors, and parent groups. (Collaboration with parents is touched upon here and expanded upon in chapter 6.)

Community Education and After-School Enrichment

Schedule culturally diverse activities after school and during summer school.

After-school enrichment and summer school classes attract and appeal to gifted learners since these classes provide opportunities to explore topics of interest and typically include in-depth activities. The opportunity to engage with peers is a bonus that can help gifted students build relationships as they immerse themselves in an area of interest. Examples of enrichment classes that engage gifted students include topics such as robotics, STEM, climate change, drama, super sleuth mystery writing, and chess, among others.

Enrichment classes can also emphasize and promote cultural diversity. They can build on students' background knowledge and experiences, allowing students to explore, share, demonstrate, and promote their unique identities and distinctive life experiences. Another benefit of enrichment classes for diverse gifted students is that they allow students to acclimate to new learning environments with other gifted students in a nonthreatening and open-minded space. After-school and summer enrichment classes can provide opportunities to meet and develop relationships with other gifted students.

Human Resources

Hire teachers of color, bilingual teachers, and culturally responsive teachers.

Research is clear that students of color derive extensive benefits when they have a teacher with whom they share a common culture (Ordway 2017). Having a teacher with whom they identify helps students feel accepted, understood, and supported. These feelings, in turn, increase students' sense of belonging, which provides numerous beneficial outcomes and leads to an increased sense of self-worth. Self-worth then transfers to higher expectations for self, increased self-confidence, and belief in oneself (Ford et al. 1994).

Human resources departments should also provide professional development in culturally responsive pedagogy as part of new-teacher training. This sends a strong message about expectations to teachers just joining the district. Presenting this message at the beginning of the school year can frame teacher mindsets and instill a sense of priority in lesson planning, instructional approach, classroom management, and parent communication.

Curriculum Department

Emphasize textbook and reading list adoptions that promote culturally responsive pedagogy.

We encourage administrators in the curriculum department to collaborate with language acquisition staff to seek materials and resources that build and support culturally responsive teaching. Use these individuals' expertise to develop a better cultural understanding of ideas and concepts portrayed in those materials. Then learn how to use the materials to develop culturally responsive pedagogy.

Having culturally sensitive materials as part of instruction in gifted classes helps learners from diverse backgrounds develop confidence. The students will likely feel better accepted and respected, which can increase their willingness to access the gifted education curriculum and instruction. It also demonstrates to the other students in the program that the newly identified learners have rich backgrounds and distinctive experiences that enrich learning for everyone.

Professional Learning Department

Prioritize professional learning opportunities for teachers and school administrators to increase cultural competencies, including culturally responsive pedagogy, antiracism, and antibias training.

In addition to adopting inclusive practices for identifying and serving diverse gifted students, schools need to refocus the professional learning opportunities provided to their teachers. Designing training to prepare educators for understanding newly identified populations of gifted learners increases teachers' awareness and competency. Suggested culturally responsive training topics include changing mindsets, antiracism, new conceptions of talent development, social and emotional sensitivities of students of color, innate abilities of diverse gifted learners, and critical race theory.

Special Education Department

Familiarize teachers who have gifted students in their classes with the attributes and learning approaches of twice-exceptional learners.

While the Naglieri General Ability Tests are not specifically designed to identify twice-exceptional (2e) students, the use of universal testing and local norms with the test trio may include 2e students in the identification pool. Based on this identification, 2e students should be included in the school's or district's gifted program. As with other special populations included in gifted services, preparing teachers to support 2e students can enhance their skills and understanding and influence their instructional approaches.

Language Acquisition

Schedule ELL teacher support for classes with bilingual gifted students.

Studies show that the new and innovative system for identifying and serving students using the Naglieri General Ability Tests intentionally and inherently identifies English language learners (Selvamenan et al. 2022). Training ELL teachers and language acquisition testers on the characteristics of gifted English language learners can help them then teach classroom teachers about students' exceptional strengths. This connection can influence teachers when they design lessons for these gifted students.

Training ELL teachers and language acquisition testers on methods for self-advocacy for gifted students who are identified using building norms can also support students' integration and comfort levels when joining gifted programs. This training can greatly support students who may feel abandoned and unsure of themselves once placed in a gifted program, as you will see in Marisol's story (see page 93). Language acquisition professionals can also support gifted English language learners by collaborating with other departments to help develop cultural awareness. Consider the characteristics of gifted English language learners on page 84 for ideas on training topics when providing professional learning opportunities.

Grants Coordinator

Access grant funds to specifically target advanced learners in Title I schools and the American Rescue Plan Elementary and Secondary School Emergency Relief (ARP ESSER) Fund under the American Rescue Plan (ARP) Act of 2021, Public Law 117-2, enacted in March of 2021.

Many schools use Title I grant funds to host after-school enrichment for students and Title II funds for providing teacher training on culturally responsive pedagogy. Schools now also have access to ESSER funds that can directly increase learning opportunities for the student groups discussed throughout this book. The ARP ESSER Fund includes three state-level reservations for activities and interventions that respond to students' academic, social, and emotional needs and address the disproportionate impact of COVID-19. There is specific language in ARP that funds should focus on underrepresented student subgroups, including each major racial and ethnic group, children from low-income families, children with disabilities, English language learners, gender, migrant students, students experiencing homelessness, and children in foster care. Unlike Title I funds that can be allocated toward traditional summer school, ESSER III provides new opportunities for gifted students in that it supports funding for comprehensive after-school programs (e.g., extended day and extended year) for those impacted by learning loss, which can also include the loss of opportunities to learn.

Equity Specialists

Inform equity specialists about the school's or district's gifted services. Provide data that documents the subgroups that are disproportionately identified and served and those that are underrepresented and underserved. Share efforts and processes in place and collaborate on ways to increase services for underrepresented populations.

The new, vastly varied, and evolving positions of equity specialist and diversity specialist are designed to bridge connections in school procedures, teacher and school administrator attention, and resources that have historically hindered equitable representation. The broad range of school-based functions that vie for these specialists' attention include gifted children who have not had access to gifted education programs for numerous reasons.

Effective gifted programs that support all gifted students rely on establishing school procedures that involve classroom placement, curriculum and instruction, academic assessments, social and emotional support, and parental involvement—all of which diversity or equity specialists can support for underrepresented gifted learners. This inclusive practice represents their role. With attention from equity specialists, schools can greatly increase access and support in gifted programs for students from underrepresented populations.

School Counselors

Provide counseling support for newly identified gifted students, especially those from underserved populations.

School counselors can guide students toward resources and support for advanced educational opportunities and help decide academic trajectories. They can significantly support newly identified gifted learners who may not have outside support or an understanding of how to navigate educational opportunities. This support could include assisting culturally and linguistically diverse students in managing social and emotional challenges that may emerge when adjusting to their gifted identification.

School Psychologists

Collaborate with the special education department to develop a system for planning classroom placement and support for students with an IEP who may also be identified as needing gifted services through universal testing.

In some states, school psychologists are required to administer an intelligence test after universal screening to determine access to gifted programs. In this situation the intelligence test used must be free of academic content to ensure that culturally and linguistically diverse students will be identified. As shown in figure 2.3 on page 20, the Cognitive Assessment System (CAS2) fits this description.

School psychologists can use the CAS2 as part of a comprehensive assessment of gifted students with very high or low scores on the Naglieri General Ability Tests who may also have a specific learning disability or other issue, such as autism spectrum disorder, ADHD, or dyslexia. School psychologists can provide instructional guidance to teachers, parents, and students themselves based on the students' cognitive processing strengths and weaknesses (Naglieri and Pickering 2010), and they can help gifted students with disabilities manage academic challenges related to their disability while in a gifted program.

Parent Groups

Collaborate with parents to build a broad and deep understanding of their gifted students' learning needs. Develop a shared vision with specific actions that can be presented to school administrators when seeking district- or school-level support.

While not an official department in a school or district, parent groups can be an important ally in building and supporting gifted services. Most parents of gifted children understand that their children have learning needs that require specialized services and support. Some parents of gifted students from diverse or underrepresented populations experience challenges when attempting to reach out to school administrators and teachers. Sometimes this is due to cultural practices, but it can also be due to educator bias. Many parents—both those whose children are successfully served in gifted programs and those whose children are not—recognize that gifted services are stronger when they support all gifted learners. Sharing information with parent groups often awakens their attention to the need to expand services to all students who would benefit from them, not just their own children.

Finding ways to reach out to parents from underserved groups can increase their awareness of gifted programs and services. Scheduling regular information meetings for parents at their home schools makes it more likely for them to attend because the home school may be closer to where families live and easier to get to and because it may feel less intimidating to attend a meeting at the home school rather than a district site. And making all the information shared in meetings easily available online ensures that parents who are unable to attend in-person due to work or child care conflicts stay informed about gifted programs and services. Those presenting the information can also fine-tune their message for the specific needs of the newly identified gifted students at the school.

Translate all parent information on the school's websites, in school newsletters, in parent resources, and at school events into parents' primary languages to encourage participation. Consider creating a gifted parent portal on the school or district website with options for English, Spanish, and other languages prevalent in the area. This approach sends an inviting message to parents who may be reluctant to seek participation in gifted programming for their children.

Collaboration with the various school departments in the district provides multiple benefits to gifted education services. Collaboration heightens awareness of the learning needs of diverse gifted learners, provides access to resources, and helps embed equitable practices throughout the entire district. It also sends a message to school personnel and the community that the school district is proactively working to build equitable and inclusive gifted services, which supports and honors student diversity.

Promoting a Sense of Belonging

There has been much discussion so far on how to academically support newly identified Black, Hispanic, and Native American students; English language learners; and students living in poverty. It is also important to consider how newly identified students might feel and how they may be perceived or treated by gifted peers and teachers—they sometimes say they feel like outsiders in their gifted program and struggle to develop a sense of belonging.

Meet Marisol

Marisol moved from Mexico to Phoenix, Arizona, where she attended school as a second-grade student. Marisol and her family spoke only Spanish, but she picked up on the English language with great speed and precocity. The language acquisition testers recognized that Marisol was an exceptional learner and nominated her for gifted testing. Marisol was identified as gifted on the Naglieri Nonverbal Ability Test when she was in second grade, her first year in the United States.

Marisol was placed in the gifted program at her school. After several years in the program, she was interviewed about her experience. Her comments and reflections were troubling. Marisol reported that she never felt accepted by her peers in the gifted program, all of whom were White. As the only Hispanic student in the program, she felt extremely alienated. She was ostracized due to her brown skin, her family's low socioeconomic status, and her lack of English proficiency. To make matters worse, students from her cultural group began excluding her from activities. They claimed that by attending the gifted classes she was trying to "act White" and "become better" than them.

Marisol began feeling extremely depressed and made attempts to discontinue her participation in the gifted program, but this was not advocated for by her parents nor changed by the school. In an attempt to fit in with her gifted peers, Marisol actually stopped speaking Spanish to her parents for a period of a year. Her siblings were forced to translate for her when she spoke with her parents and family members. She also avoided the other Hispanic students who had shunned her for participating in the gifted program.

When relating her story several years later, Marisol admitted that she had seriously considered suicide during this highly stressful time in her life. No one at the school was aware of the stress she was experiencing, and therefore, no one offered to help her manage her emotions or stepped in to improve her situation.

How many students go unnoticed like Marisol? What can be learned from her experience? What is the role of the educator in navigating situations like Marisol's and supporting students? How can educators be more aware of these troubling situations?

Embracing gifted children in their entirety—in how they think, feel, and learn—means understanding who they are and where they come from, including their racial, ethnic, and cultural background; family; community and neighborhood; and country of origin. Teachers need support in learning how to respond to unfamiliar characteristics, behaviors, and ways of being. And they need to learn what those characteristics and behaviors look like and their implications for how students learn. This is why professional development in cultural responsiveness, antibias, and antiracism is so important. Schools must also provide avenues for students to report bias, prejudice, and racism when it occurs, and they must take action when reports are made.

Some parents, like Marisol's, want their children to participate in gifted programs because they believe it will help their children obtain a level of education that the parents did not attain themselves. However, this is not true for all families. Teachers must consider that some families of newly identified students might feel very hesitant about their children taking part in what they feel are "White spaces" where they are not welcome. Families might also feel resistant when students are expected to attend a different school to participate in gifted services.

When specific and culturally sensitive academic and social and emotional interventions are in place, and when educators continually and intentionally work to support students' emotional and mental health, identification and participation in gifted programs can dramatically change the trajectory of a young person's education and future, for the better.

Contextual Considerations: Development, Environment, and Identity Group

One approach toward embracing diversity is to consider gifted children from underrepresented populations holistically within the following contexts: their development, their environment, and their identity groups. By *holistically*, we mean to look at the whole child, rather than isolating measurable aspects such as academic achievement or language proficiency or trying to determine how they "fit" into the mainstream culture. A holistic approach broadens and deepens understanding of the gifted child and can lead to personalized instruction and supports that benefit the child at school.

A holistic approach broadens and deepens understanding of the gifted child and can lead to personalized instruction and supports that benefit the child at school.

Developmental Considerations

To better understand the gifted child's development, it is important to discuss how educators' perceptions of students from underserved populations influence their expectations and instructional approaches. People's perceptions and expectations result in biases about various groups. Educators must reflect on how a student's identity influences the bias they have around the student's social development, emotional development, and cognitive development and consider what implicit biases may be clouding their vision.

A teacher's biases may be related to academics, affective traits, or behaviors, and they can impede the teacher's recognition of students' strengths. When educators have these biases, gifted students from underrepresented populations are less likely to feel accepted, resulting in a decrease in their sense of belonging and self-worth within the school system or gifted program.

Environmental Considerations

To develop awareness of gifted students' behaviors within certain contexts or environments, educators must study their students from underrepresented populations. School administrators and teachers must reflect on several aspects of student demographics: parental influence, group identity factors, the impact of the school setting, the importance of grouping gifted students together, and the importance of teacher awareness of students' cultural norms.

For example, school staff can examine how parental influence differs among the cultural groups that exist within their district. They might recognize that some Hispanic families resist having their children participate in gifted programs that are not provided at their home school, since families in many Hispanic cultures feel it important to be part of the home school community. In these cultures, parents may feel that having their child attend a gifted program that removes the student from the home school community singles the child out. This placement then interferes with that important cultural aspect. Some parents may need encouragement and information for why and how their gifted children will benefit from participating in gifted programs. Educators' sensitivity to group cultural norms will assist in this process.

Identity Group Considerations

Children relate to people from their own cultures and other identity groups. The feeling that one fits into or belongs to a group is comforting. When students have this sense of belonging, they feel accepted and encouraged, which can expand and enhance their learning opportunities and experiences. Hence, it is important to identify and group diverse gifted students with identity group peers *and* intellectual peers.

Questions to consider when thinking about how identity groups impact educators' approaches to the provision of gifted services include:

➤ What is fundamental to the identity groups present in your school, and how do these fundamentals differ for the various subgroups?

➤ Why are these identity group designations important, and how do these designations impact students' education?

➤ What misconceptions exist about the specific identity groups in your school, and how do educators' identities and personal experiences influence their views on these students' learning?

Another important question to consider is this: *What do all gifted learners have in common, and what characteristics of giftedness are unique to the various subgroups?* Some examples discussed previously are that all gifted students are quick learners, have many interests they enjoy pursuing, and enjoy learning. Ways in which they may differ in these areas may stem from having disparate backgrounds, language proficiency levels, cultural preferences and behaviors, and exposure to extended learning opportunities prior to or during their school years. These differences can be specific to identity groups as well. By creating gifted services that exclude some students based on these differences, educators overlook the commonalities that exist within the gifted population as a whole.

The activity below guides educators through these considerations as related to their school or district student populations. This exercise requires that a school or district team of teachers and school administrators focus on the students and families in their specific demographic groups to develop a deeper understanding of their students' development, environmental factors, and identity groups. The activity encourages reflection on how these elements impact the ways students learn and can help guide schools in supporting these students in gifted programs.

Teacher Workshop: Understanding Your Gifted Population

In this exercise, educators consider the gifted children from underrepresented populations in their school or district within the following contexts: development, environment, and identity group.

Development

To better understand the gifted child's development, explore how gifted students' identities impact educators and society in general.

Suggested reflections:

- Examine the ways students' cognitive growth develops given the various opportunities students have.
  - What obstacles do teachers perceive to hinder development? How can we view these perceived obstacles in a strengths-based approach to learning (i.e., building on diversity, developing cultural awareness)?
  - What supports are available in the school or school district to promote development?
- Reflect on how educator perceptions and expectations differ for specific underrepresented groups.
  - How do the students' identities impact perceptions around students' social, emotional, and cognitive development?

Environment

To draw awareness to gifted behaviors within certain contexts or environments, study the differing aspects of underrepresented populations in the school or district and how those aspects impact school behaviors. To ensure productive and helpful conversations around this topic and avoid stereotyping, be sure to discuss specific students or populations you work with. Having general conversations around this topic keeps the discussion surface-level, which can do more harm than good if the conversation turns to stereotypes.

Suggested reflections:

- Parental influence
  - How does parental influence differ among the groups?
  - How does parental influence impact gifted students at school?

- What do schools need to know about parental influence in the school's cultural groups?

◆ Group identity factors

- How do group identity factors differ among the various underrepresented groups?

- How do group identity factors impact the child at school?

◆ Impact of school setting

- How does the school setting support and honor the students' social and cultural experiences?

- What do educators need to know to better support culturally and linguistically diverse students' education?

◆ Impact of the gifted program

- Does the school community feel that gifted programs are inclusive and inviting to the school's population?

- Is entrance into the gifted program equitable for all populations in the school?

- Does participation in the gifted program reflect the school's demographics?

◆ Importance of grouping gifted students together (for at least part of every day for academics and with cultural peer groups during socialization time)

- How do the various student interactions impact students socially?

- What differences in students' interactions are noticeable among the various cultural groups?

- How do the gifted students interact when the various cultural groups are grouped together for instruction?

◆ Importance of at least one teacher being aware of the students' culture

- How does teacher awareness of students' cultures impact the social, emotional, and academic aspects of the whole gifted child?

- What outcome might this have on students' learning?

Identity Group

The whole child philosophy promotes respect for all aspects of the child. Children relate to people from their own cultures and other identity groups. Hence, it is important to identify and group diverse gifted students with both cultural and intellectual peers whenever possible.

Suggested reflections:

◆ What is fundamental with all identity groups? How do these fundamentals differ for gifted students in the various subgroups?

◆ Why are these identity group designations important? How do they impact students' education?

◆ What misconceptions exist?

◆ How do educators' identities and personal experiences influence their views on learning for students from backgrounds other than their own?

◆ How can we best respond to and serve students from underrepresented populations?

- How can we create inclusive programs after having incorporated inclusive identification procedures?

- How can we educate others about this need and necessity?

Culminating Reflections and Future Direction

Upon completing discussion on the questions noted above, it is important to map out next steps, with consideration for the thoughts and ideas that emerged from each section.

1. Break into small groups.

2. Discuss the underrepresentation of the school or school district's student populations and what you agree are the most critical and overarching tasks to initiate.

3. Based on your discussions, identify one concrete action to take within the following contexts: development, environment, and identity group.

4. Aggregate those suggestions within each of the contexts and share with the administrator who oversees gifted education in the school or district.

5. Suggest creating a small group to further plan out how and when the suggestions can be implemented.

Chapter Summary

To develop equitable gifted programs that enfranchise all gifted learners, educators must begin by acknowledging that all students with high ability need opportunities to develop their potential. The process for providing these opportunities involves recognition that some students with exceptional learning needs will take different pathways in their development than will others. When school administrators broaden their perception of who is gifted, they can then examine existing procedures and programs to determine how to develop more equitable practices that embrace and support these diverse gifted learners.

6

Culturally Responsive Approaches for Reaching and Teaching All Gifted Learners

Chapter 5 asked readers to reframe their conceptions of gifted programming to be culturally responsive to students newly identified with the Naglieri General Ability Tests. We noted that this means the new framework design for gifted programming will become organic and will develop and evolve based on the students schools identify. It also means that gifted services will differ among schools.

No single "ideal" gifted program exists, due to the varied backgrounds, cultures, and experiences of the students schools identify for participation. This holds especially true for the students we have discussed throughout the book. Ideal instruction for gifted learners follows the same philosophy as the pursuit for the ideal gifted program: no single "best" instructional plan will work for all. Rather, instructional approaches are determined by what students need, as described in this chapter.

Chapter 5 also emphasized the critical need to group students for instruction. We discussed how cluster grouping and flexible grouping practices can help teachers provide instruction that responds to students' identified needs and interests within the curriculum. This reactive approach leads us to think about designing instruction in a similarly responsive manner.

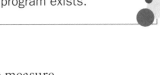

No single "ideal" gifted program exists.

We noted in chapter 2 that the goal of an ability test should be to measure how clearly a student can think to solve a problem and not what a student may or may not have learned in school. To answer the questions on the Naglieri General Abilities Tests, students identify patterns, notice sequences, recognize relationships, keep information in memory, and draw on connections they make between and within the information presented in every test item. This is the kind of thinking that is used when learning in all settings and what teachers can rely on when developing instruction for these insightful students. From this standpoint, we need to design instruction for gifted learners also based on how well the student thinks (not only on what they *know)*.

Reflective Teaching Yields Responsive Teaching

To begin our discussion of responsive classroom practices, we offer the following examples of culturally responsive teaching. In these brief vignettes, we demonstrate ways in which teachers model reflection and incorporate responsive teaching practices when working with diverse learners. Consider how you might envision and further develop these lessons for gifted learners in your classroom.

➤ In a kindergarten classroom, the teacher is reading the picture book *A Moon for Moe and Mo* by Jane Breskin Zalben. The class is discussing why it is important to celebrate all people and their cultures and backgrounds. They are learning how to celebrate and embrace the diversity within their class and how to recognize that we're all different, yet we also have so much to share and learn from one another. Strategies such as this speak directly to common characteristics of gifted children, such as their high levels of curiosity and inquiry and their heightened sense of justice, regardless of their culture or race.

➤ In a second-grade classroom, students are exploring the classroom library and choosing books for silent reading time. The selection of books includes stories from around the world and represents people of many cultures from First Nations to Nigeria to Japan. Students then share what they are reading during class discussion time. The teacher makes sure to have several culturally authentic titles that reflect the identities of his students, and also several titles that have high levels of complexity of thought and appropriately challenging language for his gifted students who are also English language learners.

➤ In a fourth-grade classroom, the students are learning about perspective and its role in shaping our perceptions of the world around us. They are working in small groups to build a concept map about perspective before beginning their William and Mary Literature Unit on perspectives. They begin the unit with each small group sharing their concept map and having whole-class discussions on the different perspectives the groups explored in this process. This interactive activity allows students to see and hear others' perspectives, which are often influenced and enriched by the students' cultures. This open-ended activity particularly appeals to gifted learners as they commonly enjoy considering information from different perspectives.

➤ In a sixth-grade classroom, the students are embarking on a global studies project, exploring the advancements of various cultures and how, through cultural borrowing, other cultures were able to learn and grow. They learn about the role of the Silk Road in spreading awareness and ideas throughout all of Asia and Europe. Next, they will start their own projects. They will create a map of their classroom's collective and individual knowledge, celebrating one another's advancements and achievements, and then embark on passion projects* that bring their learning to life.

The students determine the purpose and plan for their passion projects. This represents an excellent opportunity for them to delve into an area of interest with a historical directive. Gifted children thrive on this form of project-based learning that encourages them to build on their interests and experiences, thus resulting in broad and diverse projects the students will share with each other in the class.

➤ In a seventh-grade classroom, students are learning about global conflicts in their integrated global studies unit, where they explore wars and revolutions from multiple points of view and examine all stakeholders' perspectives. They are combining this with a literature unit on the conflict between Palestine and Israel, where they will be reading *The Shepherd's Granddaughter* by Anne Laurel Carter. Many gifted learners, including diverse gifted students, relate well to activities such as this due to their heightened sense of justice and equity, along with their desire to consider various perspectives. Studying global conflicts can also help students build awareness of and sensitivities to people from other cultures.

➤ In an eighth-grade classroom, the students are embarking on passion projects exploring civil rights and social issues. Through their interactions with one another and their topics, they are learning about the Chinese Exclusion Act and other US history, the history of South Africa and apartheid, the history of Myanmar. One group has decided to do a book study on *Efrén Divided* by Ernesto Cisneros and examine the immigration issue from multiple perspectives. Through these global histories, students are exploring the broad theme of civil rights and social issues, once again appealing to many gifted students' heightened sensitivities and deep sense of justice.

One thing all these classrooms have in common is that the teachers in them are facilitating the learning as their students are exploring the world around them through the lens of culturally relevant pedagogy. Culturally relevant pedagogy has been around for decades, but it has recently garnered renewed attention as the Black Lives Matter movement has awakened broader consciousness in society and brought more people into reflection and action to confront racism and racist systems. Yet culturally responsive teaching goes beyond being part of a social movement; it rests on how we can best teach all our students *all the time*, keeping in mind that they come from unique backgrounds and experiences and have different levels of learning.

> Culturally responsive teaching goes beyond being part of a social movement; it rests on how we can best teach all our students *all the time*.

---

*A passion project is a student-centered, project-based-learning activity, where students identify an area of interest and develop a burning question related to that topic. They then create a research project around that question and share what they learn with others.

What Is Culturally Responsive Teaching?

Culturally responsive teaching was first described by Gloria Ladson-Billings (1994) as "a pedagogy that empowers students intellectually, socially, emotionally, and politically by using cultural references to impart knowledge, skills, and attitudes" (20). Culturally responsive teaching means more than celebrating diversity according to the calendar, such as during Black History Month or on Cinco de Mayo. While employing a classroom calendar that marks all major holidays and culturally significant events is a good idea, the pursuit of creating a culturally friendly classroom community does not end by simply acknowledging events. Culturally responsive teaching not only recognizes, but celebrates and honors the heritages, cultures, and uniqueness that is contained within and outside the classroom walls. Because gifted programs have been, and continue to be, underrepresentative of some cultures and groups, this inclusive approach to teaching can be particularly relevant to newly identified gifted students.

> Culturally responsive teaching not only recognizes, but celebrates and honors the heritages, cultures, and uniqueness that is contained within and outside the classroom walls.

Culturally responsive teaching connects students' identities, languages, and life experiences with what they learn. In school, learning occurs more rapidly and efficiently when students can make connections with what they already know in life. As children grow and develop, they gain experience and background knowledge, creating hooks onto which we can attach new concepts and skills. But educators from the majority culture often unintentionally overlook the life experiences and background knowledge of learners from other cultural groups. In doing so, they miss a great opportunity to use these students' unique experiences to support their learning. When educators lack an understanding and appreciation of the nuances of cultures outside their own, they can hinder the learning potential for their students from those cultures. Culturally responsive teaching bridges this gap between teacher and student and strengthens teachers' cultural awareness.

Developing a Culturally Responsive Approach

In the foreword to Hammond (2015), Dr. Yvette Jackson asks the tough question, "Why are so many students of color underachieving?" She then answers, "This reality is a complex conundrum, requiring the need to consider and address a myriad of underregarded factors, the most prevalent being a lack of belief in the innate intellectual potential of these students. . . . If all students are wired for expansive learning and self-determination, what is needed to activate that wiring for optimal connectivity for students of color? The answer: mediating learning through culturally responsive teaching" (vi).

The world is a diverse place, and teachers are in unique positions to help students examine the many perspectives that make it up. Teachers need to make learning relevant to the students in their classrooms and the world they are a part of. This means branching away from Eurocentric* teaching and literature and making lessons more contextual and relevant to all students. For example, in a history class, try exploring various perspectives around a historical event, including those of marginalized communities. In a STEM lesson, consider technological advances in different countries and how those advancements have been influenced by the country's society and culture. Culturally responsive teaching helps students understand the relevance of other cultures and how they relate to both the past and the present.

In traditional classrooms, many teachers teach in a way similar to how they were educated. In an English language arts class, for example, teachers may default to studying the Eurocentric literature that they were exposed to in school, such as works by Shakespeare, Poe, and Mark Twain. However, there are many more perspectives and authors than these. Culturally responsive pedagogy, on the other hand, strives to include works from diverse authors and represents voices and perspectives from many cultures alongside the "classics."

In chapter 5, we defined culturally responsive pedagogy as a student-centered instructional approach that aligns with and nurtures students' unique cultural strengths to promote academic achievement while supporting and developing overall well-being. Culturally responsive pedagogy also equalizes education for all gifted populations since it draws on the experiences and strengths of all students, and not just White, affluent students.

Using Student Surveys

If student surveys are permitted in your district, they can be part of a culturally responsive approach. Using student surveys, teachers can gain personal insights, better understand students' motivations, and learn how students think and feel about themselves. This information can be invaluable in designing lessons that connect with and engage students. Using surveys sends the message that students' thoughts and feelings matter, especially when teachers use the information from the surveys in their lesson planning.

As noted previously, many times students of color, English language learners, and students living in poverty lack a sense of belonging in their gifted classes. This can hinder their participation and stifle their academic and social and emotional growth. Using results from student surveys in lesson planning naturally encourages differentiated

---

*Predominantly focusing on European culture or history, excluding a broader, more encompassing view of the world; implicitly regarding European culture as preeminent.

instruction and personalizes learning—cornerstones of learning for gifted students. It promotes student voice, respects the individual for who they are and how they feel, and builds students' self-awareness. Ultimately, these outcomes increase students' feeling of belonging and support and honor their backgrounds and identities.

We recommend conducting student surveys several times throughout the school year, since students evolve socially, emotionally, and educationally over the course of a year. Vary your questions according to the time of the year, current student concerns, specific lesson plans, or even social cues you perceive. Ask open-ended questions to draw out student reflection and voice, such as:

- How do you feel about what we are learning?

- What do you like most about our class?

- What do you like the least about our class? And how would you suggest making it better?

- What do you enjoy learning about?

- How can I better support you?

- What else would you like me to know about you?

Using student surveys can help culturally responsive teachers connect with and support their students. When acted upon, the student reflections positively contribute to teachers' instruction and students' learning. Feeling heard and respected increases the sense of belonging and improves classroom culture.

The Role of Culturally Responsive Pedagogy in the Gifted Classroom

We have noted that some students in underserved gifted populations do not feel that they belong in the gifted classes or program offered at school, since they do not see themselves represented in the student populations in these classrooms. Once placed in gifted classes, they may not feel appreciated or supported. This can be isolating, hurtful, and ultimately detrimental to students' academic progress and overall well-being.

Culturally responsive pedagogy recognizes the importance of including students' cultural identities and perspectives in all aspects of learning. Finding cultural relevance in their learning and making personal connections gives gifted students perspective, engages their prior knowledge, and provides a lens through which they can explore the content and the world around them. It gives them a voice they can use to express themselves, given their unique sensitivities and the obstacles many of them face.

Culturally responsive pedagogy is important when fostering a sense of acceptance and belonging in gifted students, especially those from culturally, linguistically, and economically diverse populations. When students feel they belong, they become empowered, which commonly leads to self-motivation and an openness to new possibilities. Students need to believe that they have a realistic chance of accessing the opportunities provided. Educators can work to break down logistical and psychological barriers to students full participation in gifted programs through purposeful selection of instructional materials, professional development for teachers, and the additional supports discussed throughout this chapter.

Examining Teachers' Perspectives and Instructional Approaches

Often, educators may think they are doing the right thing or heading in the right direction, yet in reality, they are being ineffective at best. For an example, look at the following group of middle school teachers who taught in a Title I school. They were meeting in their professional learning community (PLC) to discuss ways to help their students learn and grow. They were particularly frustrated that their students, who were from diverse backgrounds and who had varying levels of English language proficiency, were struggling academically, including the gifted students clustered into their classes.

The teachers believed that the students were not making academic growth because they were not applying themselves and that the students lacked the motivation to learn. They did not consider that there might be greater reasons underlying the students' lack of progress. They could have decided to blame the students and not make any additional efforts, but that certainly would not have addressed the issue (and would have been a harmful approach). The teachers decided to approach this dilemma within their teaching teams, with the three teacher teams tackling the problem in three different ways.

The first team decided that they needed to appeal to the students and their cultural backgrounds. They created classroom chants and started embedding rap music into their lessons, such as raps on math, history, and science. These teachers were trying to make connections to the students, and their intentions were good. Yet their approach did not go deep enough and seemed pandering. Although the lessons were engaging, the students showed little to no academic growth beyond the specific lessons associated with the chants and raps. These teachers did not get to know their students very well, nor did they tap into the underlying causes of the students' lack of academic progress.

The second team decided to start embedding lessons that celebrated Latino and African American heritage. They studied Cesar Chavez and Martin Luther King Jr. in English class, and in social studies they looked at the contributions to history that people from these heritage groups made. The second team saw some growth and were, affectively, making positive change, but these embedded lessons didn't fully embrace students' identities and backgrounds beyond initial engagement or interest. While this team's approach represented good effort, it did not go far enough to change the teachers' perspectives or mindsets and did not get to the heart of culturally responsive teaching.

The third teacher group began with the students. These teachers tried to find out more about their students: how they saw and experienced the world, how they naturally learned, and what was happening in their lives outside of school. The teachers used interest inventories, had the students journal, led classroom conversations, and incorporated teambuilding activities into daily instruction. They developed lessons that embedded personalized learning and got to know the students as they taught. They held lunch sessions with students who needed a space to talk and offered themselves as more than just deliverers of content.

This teacher group learned a great deal about each of their students, and then took the information gleaned from their lessons and classroom conversations and did additional research. They saw their students as people with complex and rich lives outside of the classroom. They realized that many of the students had little time to complete homework since they were responsible for watching their siblings or otherwise contributing to the family. The teachers learned that the students were constantly learning and engaging outside of the classroom, whether that was through watching countless YouTube and TikTok videos, helping prepare meals, sitting down to eat and converse with their family, playing games with their siblings, or listening to stories at bedtime.

These teachers learned how each of their kids perceived the world and what each child wanted to achieve. They found ways to use those connections and relationships to build a stronger classroom community, one where everyone, including the teachers themselves, could learn and grow. In these teachers' classrooms, the students started to work on passion projects and embarked on lessons that related to their interests. The teachers also integrated more of the arts into their units of study and provided choices for learning activities to students. The students had the freedom to demonstrate their knowledge in ways that were authentic for them. Ultimately, it was the students in this third teacher group who grew the most academically and affectively.

How Does Culturally Responsive Teaching Work?

A culturally responsive teaching practice develops over time. It requires a long-term commitment and must be embedded into every aspect of the teaching and learning process. It is not an engagement strategy designed to motivate or make the content relevant to students in specific groups. It is less about using students' culture as a motivator and more about discovering each student's personal and unique way of engaging in the world, including their learning styles and the ways that they acquire and produce information. This describes what we attempt to do for our gifted learners in general. However, this instructional method can help teachers learn more about their gifted learners of culturally and linguistically diverse backgrounds, specifically.

Recognizing how their students learned by seeing, by doing, through storytelling, or through interactions such as discourse and games, the teachers in the third group were able to build on their students' cultural experiences. They then used their understanding of those student experiences to relate to and support what they were teaching. The three teacher teams debriefed when they met for the next quarterly PLC meeting. They then made a plan to incorporate the most successful approach—that of the third team.

> A culturally responsive teaching practice . . . requires a long-term commitment and must be embedded into every aspect of the teaching and learning process.

You might be thinking that this is just good pedagogy, and it is. However, culturally responsive teaching also takes into consideration the ways students learn within their own cultures—whether it is through the oral histories, storytelling, and art celebrated in Latino, Native American, and Black cultures, or through the more reticent ways of discovering and processing knowledge often found in some Asian cultures. Culturally responsive teaching does not require that we explicitly tie each lesson to students' heritage and culture. Instead, it aims to interweave and honor their cultural learning experiences into instruction throughout the entire year. This approach applies students' strengths and their natural systems of gaining and processing knowledge to the classroom, and thus, helps them learn.

Culturally Responsive Teaching as a Strengths-Based Approach

Throughout this book, we have emphasized the importance of a strengths-based approach and have described ways to identify and serve gifted learners using such methods. In a strengths-based learning environment we create a classroom where each student feels as if they are an expert in some, several, or many areas. Teachers can create this environment by drawing from students' experiences and areas of expertise. Culturally responsive teaching represents a strengths-based approach: teaching to the strengths of students and through the strengths of students (Wells 2020).

In *Achieving Equity in Gifted Programming*, Wells cautions that we should be wary of attributing the perspective or experiences of a single student as being representative of their entire cultural group, given the diversity within any culture. Students need to be in learning environments in which they are free to learn without the weight of stereotype threat—the belief that their performance will be attributed to their whole group (2020). See chapter 5 for more information on students' feelings of belonging and identity.

Building Cultural Awareness

Creating culturally responsive lessons and inclusive, strengths-based instruction begins with developing cultural awareness. Educators must examine their perspectives and implicit and explicit biases about people and cultures not their own and look for areas where they have room to grow. As they get better at examining perspectives and the world around them, educators can become more aware and enlightened. This awareness can then influence the way they teach and the way they create their classroom communities. It can lead educators to use a curriculum with materials that reflect diversity, such as in photos, picture books, texts, and names consistent with the students in the school and the people in the community. This involves looking beyond just the books used in instruction. It requires that teachers consider the reading materials they provide in classroom libraries, the people and cultures they show in classroom décor, and the voices they highlight and the ones they limit in instruction (Johnson 2021).

Here are some specific examples:

➤ Instead of having only one world map with countries labeled in English, hang two maps: one English and one endonym map that has the countries labeled in the language of the countries themselves.

➤ Have posters and quotes around the classroom from people all over the world and include multilingual books in the classroom library.

➤ Create interactive bulletin boards or digital projects sharing news from around the world. Include topics with a range of complexity that gifted learners can research and study. Then have discussions about the people and societies involved in and affected by those events.

➤ Share the stories of non-White, non-affluent, and non-native-English-speaking gifted people throughout history.

Teachers have great power and opportunity to develop students' understanding and appreciation for diverse cultures. Consciously making slight adjustments in curriculum and instruction, such as in using approaches described here, can counter the insidious effects and dominating elements in society that have perpetuated in schools for far too long.

Self-Evaluating Practices

Self-evaluating practices help teachers prepare to instruct gifted learners. It is important to identify what needs to happen and how to prepare the school community to be culturally responsive within the curriculum and instructional practices. Ideally with a planning team, discuss these pertinent questions:

➤ What do you know and what do you need to learn to be effective in this practice?

➤ How do you approach making these changes?

➤ How do you institutionalize those changes throughout the community and within the school district's practices and instruction?

Answering these questions requires introspective reflection, examination of the curriculum, and community relationships.

Introspective Reflection

Reflecting on roles and personal perspectives can inform how educators teach or how administrators or districts guide educators to teach. Questions to consider include:

➤ Who do I envision as a typical "gifted learner" and why? Do some of my gifted students differ from this vision? Do my preconceived ideas of giftedness affect how I accept and welcome my students?

➤ Do I enjoy working with students who do not share my culture?

➤ Am I comfortable working with students who do not share my culture, or do I feel ill-equipped to work with these students?

➤ Do I have different expectations for some of my students? If so, are these expectations based on the strengths they exhibit or on perceived weaknesses?

➤ How do I make sure that I hold high expectations for all students, regardless of their backgrounds and cultures?

➤ What do I need to change to be effective with all my students and to ensure that all my students feel a sense of belonging, appreciation, and support?

Curriculum Examination

To determine if your curriculum is culturally relevant to students, first examine it very closely. Ideally, you will do this with a team, considering the following questions:

➤ Do the curriculum sources I use feature multiple perspectives and points of view?

➤ Does the curriculum reflect multiple cultures, including some not represented by the students?

➤ Does the curriculum challenge and promote critical-thinking and problem-solving skills for all students?

➤ Is the curriculum appropriately rigorous for all students?

Keep in mind that a curriculum in and of itself is not culturally responsive; it depends on what the teachers do with it. When planning or reflecting on a lesson, also reflect on the instructional approach. Ask these questions:

➤ Have multiple viewpoints been shared and discussed?

➤ Are the authors of my curriculum diverse?

➤ How have I ensured that all students are interested, challenged, and motivated?

➤ How have I ensured that the curriculum is relevant and explores the diverse experiences and perspectives of the students in my classroom as well as people outside it?

➤ Do I use a range of instructional strategies connected to the strengths and needs of all my students?

Community Relationship Building

Building community relationships is critical for developing inclusive gifted services and instruction. Bearing in mind that the existing practices for serving gifted students have long histories in many school districts, consider what has been overlooked or neglected in the past. The need for these considerations pertains to all stakeholder groups: school administrators, teachers, parents, and all other school personnel. Reflections in these areas are equally important in all districts, whether the district is urban, suburban, or rural, and whether it is small, medium, or large. Questions to consider include:

- ➤ What do we need to learn about our families' cultures, situations, and family structures?

- ➤ How can we build relationships with our families? Whose support do we need to make this happen?

- ➤ What is the foundation we are building upon and what message have we been sending to our school community? What message do we want to be sending?

- ➤ Does our school administration recognize and support community-building efforts?

- ➤ How are we reaching out to families to share information about gifted identification, programming, and instruction?

- ➤ Which departments or school administrators can we appeal to for help in supporting our efforts?

- ➤ What information do we need to share for these administrators to appreciate the need for their support?

Planning Activity

Collaborate with grade-level teams, cluster teacher teams, or in PLCs to answer these questions. List the positive changes you have already made and the things you are doing right. Think about ways to build on that success. Then, brainstorm things you or your team can do in the areas and practices that need improvement.

Learning About Your Students: A Starting Point

When preparing to implement and lead a plan to reach a diverse group of gifted learners, begin by identifying starting points and asking some thoughtful questions of the planning group. Consider creating a teacher survey including the following questions to gather information, and then analyze this feedback:

➤ Have you determined the strengths, needs, and interests of your students?

➤ Have you conducted an interest inventory or incorporated affective education into your classroom?

➤ Have you asked students what they need from you and from the classroom environment to be successful?

When teachers endeavor to understand students and establish relationships with them, they are better able to serve students' unique needs and adopt student-centered approaches.

Educators regularly examine how to respond to the learning differences of gifted students. This is where culturally responsive teaching comes in. It provides a framework for teachers to see students for who they are and to embrace this uniqueness to enrich their academic experiences and skills. A culturally responsive approach provides an avenue to bring students' cultures into the classroom and demonstrates to students that who they are matters.

We cannot talk about being culturally responsive without thinking about what is going on in the world, the nation, and our students' communities. Educators need to be aware of how societal events and ingrained systems impact the students in their classrooms and gifted programs. Teachers, administrators, and education professionals must acknowledge this impact and provide safe environments in which students can explore the nuances of the world and its effect on their lives. This reflection is especially important with gifted students, since many have a strong sense of justice and fairness and an acute awareness of the inequities in the world.

> Educators need to be aware of how societal events and ingrained systems impact the students in their classrooms and gifted programs.

Expanding Perspectives Through Content

Culturally responsive teaching is embedded in the principles of academic success, cultural competence, and sociopolitical consciousness (Ladson-Billings 1994). In this section, we provide examples of how teachers can use these principles to expand students' global perspectives throughout the content areas. We also share characteristics of educators effective in teaching diverse gifted students following these principles. These content-area snippets are intended to spark ideas for how you can embed these principles and perspectives into your curriculum and instruction. By appealing to the ideas, insights, and interests of diverse gifted learners, teachers can foster engagement in ways that reach beyond the standard curriculum.

Arts

The arts encompass all artistic expressions, from dance, to music, to media arts, and beyond. The term *art* as used here is meant to be all-inclusive, encapsulating the many forms. Art is a wonderful and natural way to examine global perspectives and celebrate diverse cultures. Academic success is embedded into arts curriculum either through teaching the skills necessary to complete the work or through using art as a medium to explore the learning. Cultural competence is fostered through exploring artists who have made vast and significant contributions to the world and learning about their history and how they affected their communities.

Art can be included in regular classroom practices in a variety of ways, such as in response to what the class is studying or what books they are reading, in relation to a calendar celebration, or in response to current events. Arts and cultural integration can also take various forms. Students can perform dances or songs that have meaning to them or their culture. They can create works of art that exhibit their thoughts and feelings on complex topics or showcase a particular perspective, person, or event. They can put on short plays or skits that highlight fables and folktales of the cultures represented in the room.

Art can also be embedded into all forms of instruction, from math to writing to affective education. Integrating the arts into regular school curriculum is important for all students. For gifted students who may not be able to fully express themselves through language, the arts provide a less restrictive form of expression that incorporates their cultures and strengths.

Literature

Culturally responsive teaching in literature extends past the texts into how teachers are teaching and how students are reaching academic success. It is the educator's job to help all students grow as critical thinkers. Consider how students solved the verbal items on the Naglieri General Ability Tests. They did not rely on words, but on their understanding of verbal concepts using critical-thinking skills.

Nigerian novelist Chimamanda Ngozi Adichie, in her 2009 TED Talk "The Danger of a Single Story," spoke of how she grew up reading British and American children's literature and how they influenced her writing as a student, stating: "I wrote exactly the kinds of stories I was reading: All my characters were white and blue-eyed, they played in the snow, they ate apples . . . and they talked a lot about the weather, how lovely it was that the sun had come out. . . . My characters also drank a lot of ginger beer, because the characters in the British books I read drank ginger beer. . . . Now, I loved those American and British books I read. They stirred my imagination. They opened up new worlds for me. But the unintended consequence was that I did not know that people like me could exist in literature." She tells the audience this to highlight what happens when students are only shown a limited perspective, one that does not represent the rest of the world, or worse, does not represent them. The Cooperative Children's Book Center (CCBC), a research library of the University of Wisconsin–Madison School of Education, reported that in 2019, only 11 percent of the total children's books published were about backgrounds and experiences other than those of White children, and over 83.3 percent of the published children's books were written or illustrated by White authors and illustrators (2021). This has a significant impact on students, as illustrated by Adichie's perspective. If students are to be successful in a multicultural world, then they must learn from and about multiple perspectives, and they must feel encouraged to express themselves freely within their own cultural norms.

So often literature curriculum is derived from the traditional Western canon; however, there are many more voices and perspectives that should be considered. One can embed deep explorations of poems and speeches from prominent African Americans, such as Paul Laurence Dunbar, Langston Hughes, Maya Angelou, and Dr. Martin Luther King Jr., including context about the time in which they were written and discussing how these works are relevant today. Similarly, you can include works by Hispanic children's book authors such as Sandra Cisneros, Pat Mora, Pam Muñoz Ryan, and Gary Soto, whose storytelling provides strong cultural connections for many students.

> In 2019, only 11 percent of the total children's books published were about backgrounds and experiences other than those of White children, and over 83.3 percent of the published children's books were written or illustrated by White authors and illustrators.

Teachers can seek out books that have been nominated for or won awards such as the Coretta Scott King Award, the American Indian Youth Literature Award, the Robert F. Sibert Informational Book Medal, the Orbis Pictus Award, and the Pura Belpré Award.* Consider diverse authors, perspectives, characters, and settings (for example, *Sal and Gabi Break the Universe* by Carlos Hernandez) when reading about mythology, and include mythology other than Greek and Roman. *My Beautiful Birds* by Suzanne Del Rizzo, *The Other Side: Stories of Central American Teen Refugees Who Dream of Crossing the Border* by Juan Pablo Villalobos, and *Refugee* by Alan Gratz would be excellent choices for including refugee studies and perspectives in the social studies curriculum. A nonfiction book, such as *Titanosaur: Discovering the World's Largest Dinosaur* by Drs. José Luis Carballido and Diego Pol, illustrated by Florencia Gigena, about a paleontological dig in Argentina, or *The Boy Who Harnessed the Wind* by William Kamkwamba and Bryan Mealer, about a boy in Malawi who produces electricity from found items, are examples of multicultural nonfiction texts that can be used to support concepts taught in a science class.

Literature is naturally embedded within the culture that created it, and it is a reflection of that culture's or author's perspective. For example, *We Are Grateful: Otsaliheliga*, written by Traci Sorell and illustrated by Frané Lessac, is a nonfiction book about Cherokee gratitude, celebrations, and experiences. Teaching students to read for these ideas and perspectives helps them learn how to write with the

*The Coretta Scott King Award is dedicated to outstanding African American authors of children's books that show appreciation of African American culture and universal human values; the American Indian Youth Literature Award recognizes outstanding contributions to children's literature by and about Native Americans; the Robert F. Sibert Informational Book Medal is awarded to the most distinguished informational book; the Orbis Pictus Award promotes and recognizes excellence in the writing of nonfiction for children; and the Pura Belpré Award is presented to Latino and Latina writers and illustrators whose work best portrays, affirms, and celebrates the Latino cultural experience in an outstanding work of literature for children and young people.

same goal and purpose. The students may then become advocates for equity and diversity.

To develop cultural competence, educators can look at the examples described through literature above. Teachers can also encourage the asking of questions in a Socratic Seminar or Harkness Circle* about whose voices are being represented and whose are not. Sociopolitical consciousness can be fostered through conversations held in class, but also through the subject matter of the texts students read.

Math

Within math instruction, culturally responsive teaching asks educators to consider the student's role in the math classroom. Are students absorbers of knowledge who are asked only to apply formulas, or are they critical thinkers who have their own perspectives and ways of solving mathematical problems? How are lessons, learning opportunities, and assessments structured to ensure success for all students as they engage in mathematical sense-making and reasoning? According to Dr. Mark Ellis (2019), culturally responsive mathematics teaching (CRMT) "is about inviting all students into mathematics as competent participants whose ways of thinking and reasoning are worth sharing, discussing, and refining. Most of all, it's about ensuring each and every learner not only has success with mathematics, but also comes to see mathematics as a tool for examining their world" (6).

Culturally responsive mathematics teaching still focuses on teaching mathematical concepts and skills and developing proficiency; however, it extends beyond these goals to connect math to authentic use and apply it to current issues. Importantly, as pertaining to diverse gifted students, this method engages students' identities by honoring their prior experience, their communities, and their individuality. CRMT's success lies in establishing a learning environment in which each student feels valued for who they are and for their individual and collective contributions to the success of the classroom community (Aguirre and Zavala 2013; Ladson-Billings 1995; 2009; 2014).

This approach could be constructed as a problem-based-learning opportunity where students examine statistics that affect the community. You might begin by creating an interest survey so students can share about the real-world topics they would like to explore in math class. In a self-contained gifted class or learning environment, the teacher can tie the project to current events students are learning about in social studies and in research projects they are doing in science and writing. Once you have developed potential topics, have a class discussion to create a focus question. Consider: "What might the big question be and what data are needed to effectively answer it?" Next, determine the math skills and concepts that are needed and which of those skills and concepts must be learned. From here, teach students the embedded skills while writing the project.

---

*Socratic Seminars represent formal discussion, based on a text, in which the leader asks open-ended questions. Within the context of the discussion, students listen closely to the comments of others and articulate their own critical thinking, offering their thoughts and responses. In Harkness Circles, every student in the class questions, contributes, and contemplates to learn, succeed, and receive a grade.

Help students construct mathematical arguments and develop their mathematical reasoning, all while facilitating critical thinking and honoring what each child brings to the task, as well as their unique perspective. Finally, consider working with the students in developing how they would like to showcase their learning. By having open-ended focus questions and student-directed authentic learning opportunities, you are honoring the process for each student regardless of their achievement levels in the math content you are teaching.

Science, Technology, and Engineering

Culturally relevant teaching in science focuses on the same premise as other content areas; the goals are to make content engaging and relevant to students' lives and enable them to achieve a higher level of learning and academic success. By providing hands-on, inquiry-based science experiments, projects, and lessons, teachers strive to reach each and every student. Some science practices that embrace culturally responsive teaching include traditional events, such as participating in science fair competitions where students research and conduct experiments on topics of interest to them. Students can also embark on problem-based-learning projects such as those working with renewable energy, cleaning up their community, or in programs such as Cubes in Space, where they research problems and create potential solutions.

If students have interest in technology or engineering, they could create apps and computer programs that solve a problem, or they could work with urban planning units to learn how infrastructure helps society. In these projects, students are bringing their passion and desire to learn to their work. They are learning the scientific principles needed to succeed in the project and embarking on authentic research. Science, technology, and engineering offer gifted learners opportunities to study and research topics of interest that are not heavily reliant on language. Many of these cross a variety of cultures, allowing for a broad range of contextual understandings.

Social Studies

Social studies classes or lessons are an excellent platform for connecting what is happening in the world today with what has happened in the past. But culturally responsive teaching need not be limited to history lessons. Students can write research pieces and create documentaries or podcasts about specific events with which they have personal connections, whether those are through their cultural experiences or current interests.

Lessons in civics and history are ripe with opportunities to examine multiple perspectives. In a civics lesson, you could use the book *V Is for Voting* by Kate Farrell and illustrated by Caitlin Kuhwald, wherein each letter stands for a word related to civics and social studies. Using the letter *G*—"G is for govern: to lead and to guide"—you can teach a class on what it means to lead and guide. In a middle school or high school classroom, try combining this picture book with a study on Martin Luther King Jr., a reflection of a leader and his call to action for all people. Once you progress to *H*—"H is for homelands that we've occupied"—a discussion on the history of exploration and imperialism can take place. Another civics lesson idea is to use *Lifting as We Climb: Black Women's Battle for the Ballot Box* by Evette Dionne or *The Teachers March! How Selma's Teachers Changed History* by Sandra Neil Wallace and Rich Wallace, and illustrated by Charly Palmer, as a mentor text to guide a conversation about fighting for civil rights. These stories might inspire students from many cultures to explore civil rights movements in countries to which they connect.

Writing

The act of writing provides a way for students to explore, analyze, and address the world in which they live. Therefore, writing instruction should foster this goal. Writing is a powerful tool in which one can express oneself and convey a message to one's intended audience (Ladson Billings 2014; Winn and Johnson 2011). It is also adaptable and can be utilized for myriad purposes in different contexts. Writing can spur others to consider perspectives that facilitate change.

Powerful orators began by honing their craft of writing. Consider the works and impact of speakers such as Frederick Douglass, Tupac Shakur, Maya Angelou, Amanda Gorman, or Mahatma Gandhi; classical writers such as William Shakespeare, Jane Austen, Mary Wollstonecraft, Charles Darwin, and Plato; and politicians like Nelson Mandela, Winston Churchill, and Abraham Lincoln. All these people had the power to craft language to fulfill a purpose and communicate complex ideas and emotions. Their writings helped create movements and facilitate change.

In the classroom, teachers have the power to help students explore and understand the world and discover their voices. As students begin to *learn to* read and write, they grow to *learn from* reading and writing. Writing, therefore, is a tool for learning and communication, and the ability to effectively communicate through writing is one of the most important skills that students must learn. However, many students lack the requisite skills, which leaves them at a disadvantage in school and in society. Graham (2008) asserts that there is a direct correlation with performance in writing and performance in other subject areas. According to a 2017 NAEP report, only 27 percent of fourth-, eighth-, and twelfth-grade students are proficient in writing. While this is already concerning, the same report demonstrates that there is a larger underperformance in African American and Hispanic students who scored, on average, 18 points below the benchmark score, and 6 points below the average of their White counterparts. This is a troubling trend that highlights the need to create a classroom environment in which writing is ubiquitous with the learning process and celebrated in all its forms.

In the culturally responsive classroom, teachers embrace the strengths and perspectives of the students while providing feedback and instruction to help them grow in the different content areas. One way to do this in relation to writing is to include a writer's workshop in the classroom. In this way, students are always writing and honing their craft, yet not everything they produce must be submitted for assessment. Another practice that can help students grow their writing skills is to consider the many types of writing that exist and promote those that appeal most to students. For example, students can create their own comics, graphic novels, podcasts, plays, songs, poems, speeches, debates, stories, and other creative writing pieces, in addition to the traditional research papers and reports. Having options such as these can be particularly motivating for gifted learners who may not be proficient English speakers, as these options can help gifted English language learners engage and interact in ways that encourage and invite their participation and exploration.

Consider students' strengths and interests outside of writing and find ways to include them in the writing process, remembering that writing is a form of expression. Students can craft poems that express their experiences and perspectives. They can generate stories that are either embedded in fiction or nonfiction to express themselves. They can create videos to teach others about their cultures and experiences and post them on TikTok and YouTube, or they can create stop-motion movies or code video games to explore and teach concepts to their peers or younger students.

Consider incorporating writing into other subject areas as well. This approach makes writing authentic and a natural part of the learning process. In a culturally responsive classroom, writing instruction is centered around students' thinking and experiences, which can at times expose injustices, communicate issues and problems, and promote activism (Coker and Lewis 2008). Have students use writing to facilitate change, writing speeches or crafting letters to politicians. Above all, ensure that writing instruction is authentic, powerful, and contingent on the experiences, strengths, and interests of students (Christensen 2017; Ife 2012; and Kahn 2009).

Commonalities in and Across Content Areas

Teachers who approach instruction in a culturally inclusive manner as described in the scenarios above generally share some common characteristics in their teaching practices, regardless of their content area. Many also exhibit some common traits or use methodologies such as those listed next. While these teaching methodologies are important for all students, they are particularly important for students from historically marginalized communities who are often overlooked in classroom learning experiences and instruction, as well as in pedagogy and curriculum. Effective teachers of diverse gifted learners recognize gifted potential in all populations and often do the following (Winebrenner and Brulles 2018):

➤ support students' social and emotional needs by learning how these differ among diverse student populations

➤ recognize and respond to students who need learning accommodations and modifications

➤ compact curriculum, differentiate instruction, and form flexible learning groups

➤ integrate basic skills with higher-order-thinking skills

➤ create and use learning extensions and tiered lessons to scaffold instruction

- incorporate ongoing use of formative assessments to gauge students' academic progress
- develop students' ability to use self-directed learning
- build effective parent-teacher partnerships

These traits and methodologies may also serve as professional learning topics for staff members when working to adopt more culturally responsive instructional approaches and inclusive mindsets.

In addition to supporting teachers in developing these traits and methods, review the *CRSE Steam Curriculum Score Card Guidelines* (Peoples, Islam, and Davis 2021) for recommendations to support teachers in a culturally responsive instructional approach. A few of these recommendations include providing guidance on:

- using students' everyday lives as the starting point for learning
- making real-life connections between academic content and students' cultures, environments, community issues, and current events
- creating opportunities to meaningfully engage students' families to enhance lessons
- demonstrating inclusion of an array of possible student responses
- designing lessons or engaging in conversations that disrupt power inequities or create opportunities for students to consider alternatives

Once again, these recommendations can serve all students. But with the newly identified diverse group of gifted learners, it is important to connect how those with high ability think and process information. We have discussed how gifted learners think critically, probe with their questions, and make complex connections while also drawing on past experiences. Making learning personal and giving students opportunities to self-direct engages and motivates those with high ability. Teachers accomplish this by building on the students' background experiences and intellectual strengths.

Culturally Responsive Assessment Strategies

Another common practice that can lead to inequity is seen in schools' grading policies. These inequities in assessing learning can be seen in diverse and historically marginalized student groups, and within the gifted students represented in those groups. Educators must question what they are really measuring with grades and who those grades are serving. If the purpose of assignments is to foster learning, then educators must first determine what will lead to this goal and what will not. *Then* they can plan how that learning will be assessed.

The system of traditional assessment many teachers use is often based on their own school experiences. In this system, students learn a new lesson, skill, or task in one week and are assessed to determine if they have mastered the skill on that Friday. They are assigned a grade for the assessment, and then the class moves on to the next learning target. In many cases, this leaves no room for remediation if students haven't yet mastered the skill. Nor is there room for students to extend past the content if they have already mastered the learning target.

When gifted students must work to demonstrate mastery to receive a grade, many experience diminished interest in what they are learning. And when their interest is not piqued, gifted students commonly take the easiest possible path to achieve a desired grade. In this scenario, the paradigm shifts from learning to completing a task for a grade. Students' critical thinking is reduced, and they become less engaged in the learning process. Gifted students who face additional hurdles, such as not being proficient in English or lacking background knowledge needed to build mastery on the skill being assessed, may not put forth the effort necessary to succeed in the task.

> When gifted students must work to demonstrate mastery to receive a grade, many experience diminished interest in what they are learning.

To encourage gifted learners to take academic risks, assessments must be meaningful to them. We have discussed the importance of authentic and responsive learning opportunities. But it is important to extend this mindset to authentic testing, especially for diverse gifted learners. Accomplishing this goal begins with determining what the desired learning targets are, why those targets are important, and what mastery looks like for a specific student. (Surely not quick and easy, but a worthy task!)

Preassessments

Preassessing is key to the process of authentic learning and assessment. Preassessment determines what each student already knows and to what degree they have mastered a skill or concept. This is especially important with gifted learners, given their complex natures and varied learning experiences. When creating preassessment plans, teachers can ask, "What are the students' roles in the assessment process? What are the teachers' roles? How might these approaches differ with the diverse learners within the classroom?"

Gifted learners are not a homogeneous group; they have different backgrounds and perspectives. Therefore, make an effort to solicit input from your students about what course elements do or do not foster learning for them. Prior to administering preassessments, determine if the goal is the process of learning or the final grade. This consideration is key in developing intrinsic motivation (for learning) as opposed to extrinsic motivation (for receiving a grade). The distinction between the two can be a major motivating factor in gifted students' learning engagement.

Rethinking Roles in Assessing Learning

Help students develop their learning goals for the year, semester, quarter, or week with a focus on growth over mastery. This can be very rewarding for gifted learners, who can often demonstrate mastery easily without experiencing academic growth. Gifted students enjoy learning and typically recognize their own growth and progress.

Asking students to develop detailed plans for learning and growth in their own words, using learning targets and preassessment data, motivates them to take on new learning challenges. In this process, students need to articulate where they are starting and where they hope to end up with their learning, reflect on what is achievable and realistic, and determine what they are going to do to achieve their goal. Having them revisit and reflect on these plans at least weekly embeds the process and strengthens the achievement outcomes. This personalized process can help gifted learners reflect on and care about what they produce and celebrate their growth and successes, no matter how small.

We encourage educators to rethink their role as they work with students and help them achieve their goals. In this evolved role, teachers encourage practice, provide timely and actionable feedback, and demonstrate that they are equally invested in their students' learning as a partner in the experience. This approach demonstrates respect for the students and helps build student confidence.

Authentic assessments might include providing an audience for students' learning. This can be done through project-based or community-enhanced learning, in a showcase, in an academic competition, in a professional mentoring program, in a partnership with the community on an action research project, or in writing to legislators or the school board. When working with diverse gifted learners to determine how they should be assessed, consider providing choice for the way students will demonstrate growth, such as with portfolios where they can showcase products of their choice that achieve their goals.

Applying Culturally Responsive Practices

Recall the student scenarios from chapter 4 (page 64):

Isabella:
Achievement scores: Language arts 90th percentile; Math 82nd percentile
Ability scores: Standard scores, Verbal = 110, Quantitative = 100, Nonverbal = 102

Angel:
Achievement scores: Language arts 75th percentile; Math 99th percentile
Ability scores: Standard scores, Verbal = 120, Quantitative = 135, Nonverbal = 130

Alex:
Achievement scores: Language arts 99th percentile; Math 99th percentile
Ability scores: Standard scores, Verbal = 132, Quantitative = 130, Nonverbal = 135

Isabella's Naglieri General Ability Tests scores showed that her current level of instruction was sufficiently challenging and that she did not need gifted services. Although Isabella's and Angel's *achievement* scores did not differ drastically, Angel's *ability* test scores showed a need for gifted services at a basic to moderate level. Alex scored highly for achievement and at the highest levels for ability and requires gifted services.

We now describe how a teacher might design instruction for Isabella, Angel, and Alex in a given lesson.

Isabella

Isabella is a third-grade Latina student whose needs can be served in a general education classroom; however, she would benefit from being given additional challenges in the areas of her strengths, and especially in content she has already demonstrated mastery in, such as some aspects of English language arts. Isabella's teacher can give her (and all the students in the classroom) preassessments to determine what she has already mastered in the units of study and then provide opportunities for enrichment and choice to help extend her thinking and learning.

Angel

Angel, a fifth-grade Black student in a large urban district with a very high level of poverty, shows potential above his grade-level peers and is in need of specialized services. Since he earns A's in subjects that are of interest to him, but has difficulties in subjects that do not hold his interest, it will be important for his teacher to assess Angel's interests to guide instruction. As was recommended to Isabella's teacher, Angel's teacher can preassess all students in the class prior to embarking on units of study. This will ensure that students like Angel are not idling through instruction and will help engage them in the lessons and in school.

Angel's quantitative score on the Naglieri General Ability Tests and his performance in math indicate that this is consistently a strong subject for him, and one that motivates him. His verbal score of 120 also indicates that he has potential that is greater than his current language arts achievement level, a subject that is of less interest to him. When we look at Angel's profile (verbal, nonverbal, and quantitative scores), we can see that he needs to be given a challenge, and that he would benefit greatly from culturally responsive teaching. To be more culturally responsive, Angel's teacher can use Angel's strengths, perspectives, and interests to help him be successful in all academic areas. Angel's teacher can create opportunities to learn more about him and can find ways to help him look at school differently.

Using an interest inventory, the teacher can see Angel's other areas of interest and can combine them with language arts instruction. Perhaps through the inventory, the teacher finds that Angel is interested in video games. This interest could be combined with Angel's love of math and his ability to see and understand patterns into a project where, for example, he creates a video game to showcase his knowledge of a book that he has read.

Angel's teacher can combine passion projects, choice, and problem-based learning to not only allow Angel to build on his strengths, but also to use them to support his areas of needed growth. Angel's teacher can approach teaching him as a partnership to discover who Angel is and all the wonderful ways he learns, engages with learning, and imparts knowledge.

Alex

Alex is a White, highly gifted kindergarten student in a rural school district who also lives in poverty. His school offers few diversified learning experiences. Nevertheless, Alex has academic needs that are vastly different from his age-level peers. He needs radical acceleration in several subjects. Various options should be considered, including grade skipping, enrollment in multiage classrooms, and content acceleration. Single content area acceleration in math and reading could be beneficial, but to what degree must be determined by preassessment. The content area acceleration could be provided in a few ways, from individualized acceleration plans, to having an aide work with the other students as the teacher works with Alex on higher-level skills, or even to pushing Alex into upper grades for specific lessons. Alex can be given preassessments in all units of instruction and should only be expected to participate in lessons where there is knowledge he has not yet mastered or when there are enrichment opportunities that extend past his current mastery.

As he is already reading chapter books, Alex has likely also mastered all aspects of reading instruction for this age, which should be determined and documented. If it is reading aloud time, he should still listen, but the teacher should ask him questions with more depth and complexity to engage and challenge him. If the students are practicing reading, he can have silent reading time. He will still benefit from participating in group activities, since his affective needs can likely be met with his age-level peers, but he will probably have interests that are quite different from those of his classmates.

Culturally responsive teaching honors the experiences of all students and builds a classroom community where different perspectives are celebrated. Alex's teachers can offer him opportunities for extension, exploration, and choice as often as possible. He should not be graded using the same assessment measures as his peers, especially considering he has already mastered the content, and he does not need to participate in class since the work has no interest or benefit for him. This does not excuse him from learning, however. Instead, he can be given different ways to learn, demonstrate knowledge, and be assessed, based on his personal growth and learning.

Chapter Summary

In this final chapter, we sought to bring the identification, service, and instructional processes full circle by emphasizing what we started with in chapter 1: an understanding that our long-held, traditional approaches toward identifying and serving diverse gifted students are not working for all gifted students and that instructional approaches for serving these learners can be improved. With the Naglieri General Ability Tests, the gifted population identified is expanding to be more diverse and equitable. It follows that our gifted programs and classroom instruction must then also become more inclusive and culturally responsive.

Ending systems that lead to inequity and underrepresentation in gifted programs requires that we look beyond just the identification process and into the classroom. We recognize that the problem of inequity is often further perpetuated once students from marginalized populations enter gifted programs.* Plucker et al. (2017) argue that, to be inclusive of underrepresented populations, a program must modify its options and/or its gifted classrooms to appeal to these advanced students. This occurs when educators examine their personal biases and ensure their curriculum is culturally relevant and addresses the needs of all their gifted learners.

In this chapter, we have demonstrated why and how culturally responsive teaching and pedagogy are important transformative teaching practices that benefit all students, and especially underrepresented gifted learners. The processes we discussed involve attention to all social variations and backgrounds, including students' cultures, socioeconomic groups, genders, linguistic backgrounds, and ability levels. When integrated into classroom instruction for gifted learners, culturally responsive pedagogy promotes equity and inclusivity in the classroom, engages students in the course material while supporting their critical-thinking skills, and ultimately strengthens students' sense of belonging and identity. Effective teaching using this construct requires ongoing professional development in antibias and antiracist mindsets. With these mindsets, we can begin to create inclusive classrooms that reflect culturally responsive teaching for all gifted learners.

Throughout the chapter, we have emphasized the creation of an environment where an expanded mindset is celebrated and everyone is invested in one another. In this safe environment, we can teach students how to celebrate their individuality as well as their collective successes. Students feel more comfortable accepting new challenges, pursuing their interests, and building upon their unique background knowledge and experiences.

*Research shows that Black, Hispanic, and Native American students are more likely to drop out of gifted programs than their White and Asian peers (Ecker-Lyster and Niileksela 2017; Ford 2012a, 2012b, 2014a, 2014b; Grantham 2004).

A Final Note

In the introduction to this book, we asked you to reflect on your interpretation and understanding of diversity, equity, and inclusion in the context of the gifted services used in your school. You read about how longstanding testing and teaching practices have perpetuated inequity, the origins of those erroneous methods, and new ways to ensure and provide opportunities for historically underrepresented gifted students. Reading the book, you likely reflected on how your school's, your district's, and your own practices may hinder progress in identifying and serving Black, Hispanic, and Native American students; English language learners; and students living in poverty in gifted programs.

As noted in the introduction, the goal of this book is to demonstrate ways educators can identify and serve the over one million gifted students who were not identified and were not given the opportunity to participate and thrive in gifted education programs. Accomplishing this goal demands that we incorporate equitable ability tests and use inclusive program models and culturally responsive teaching methods that reflect changing mindsets and new practices. This goal necessitates that educators closely examine students' abilities from a strengths-based perspective and within the context of their school's student population.

It is critically important to recognize that equitable identification of gifted students can be achieved only through equitable assessment practices. Each part of the process must be equitable to achieve equitable outcomes. As was noted in the *McFadden vs. Board of Education for Illinois School Distrtict U-46* court case, even though a fair nonverbal measure of ability was used (the NNAT), the requirement that all students have high verbal and quantitative achievement test scores blocked Hispanic students' access to the gifted program. We urge readers to be mindful of all the possible obstacles for underrepresented students in the assessment process. Then, after identifying students for services based in part on the Naglieri General Ability Tests, use the scores as part of an equitable assessment process and use inclusive school practices, while proactively providing professional learning opportunities to broaden school staff's view of students' needs and strengths.

In closing, bear in mind why you entered education: to help all children learn. To do this, it is important to recognize each student's potential and ensure they receive an equitable and appropriate education. This is the responsibility of all educators, and we hope this book can serve as a helpful guide on the road to accomplishing this goal. We *can* do better, and we *must*!

References

Adichie, Chimamanda Ngozi. 2009. "The Danger of a Single Story." TED. Accessed March 23, 2022. ted.com/talks/chimamanda_ngozi_adichie_the_danger_of_a_single_story.

AERA, APA, and NCME. 2014. *Standards for Educational and Psychological Testing*. Washington, DC: AERA Publications.

Aguirre, Julia M., and Maria del Rosario Zavala. 2013. "Making Culturally Responsive Mathematics Teaching Explicit: A Lesson Analysis Tool." *Pedagogies: An International Journal* 8 (2): 163–190. doi.org/10.1080/1554480X.2013.768518.

American Psychological Association. 2021. "Apology to People of Color for APA's Role in Promoting, Perpetuating, and Failing to Challenge Racism, Racial Discrimination, and Human Hierarchy in the U.S." October 29, 2021. apa.org/about/policy/racism-apology.

Avant, Anna, and Marcia O'Neal. 1986. "Investigation of the Otis-Lennon School Ability Test to Predict WISC-R Full Scale IQ for Referred Children." Paper presented at the Annual Meeting of the Mid-South Educational Research Association (15th, Memphis, TN). November 19–21, 1986. files.eric.ed.gov/fulltext/ED286883.pdf.

Brulles, Dina. 2018. "The Whole Gifted Child Task Force: Report to the NAGC Board of Directors." March 2018. bit.ly/NAGC_WGC.

Brulles, Dina, and Karen Brown. 2018. *A Teacher's Guide to Flexible Grouping and Collaborative Learning: Form, Manage, Assess, and Differentiate in Groups*. Minneapolis, MN: Free Spirit Publishing.

Brulles, Dina, Rachel Saunders, and Sanford Cohn. 2010. "Improving Performance for Gifted Students in a Cluster Grouping Model." *Journal for the Education of the Gifted* 34 (2): 327–350. files.eric.ed.gov/fulltext/EJ910197.pdf.

Brulles, Dina, and Susan Winebrenner. 2019. *The Cluster Grouping Handbook: How to Challenge Gifted Students and Improve Achievement for All (Revised and Updated Edition)*. Minneapolis, MN: Free Spirit Publishing.

Canivez, Gary, Marley W. Watkins, and Stefan C. Dombrowski. 2017. "Structural Validity of the Wechsler Intelligence Test for Children—Fifth Edition: Confirmatory Factor Analyses with the 16 Primary and Secondary Subtests." *Psychological Assessment* 29: 458–472.

Carballido, José Luis, and Diego Pol. 2019. *The Titanosaur: Discovering the World's Largest Dinosaur*. New York: Orchard Books.

Carman, Carol, Christine Walther, and Robert Bartsch. 2018. "Using the Cognitive Abilities Test (CogAT) 7 Nonverbal Battery to Identify the Gifted/Talented: An Investigation of Demographic Effects and Norming Plans." *Gifted Child Quarterly* 62 (2): 193–209.

Carter, Anne Laurel. 2008. *The Shepherd's Granddaughter*. Toronto: Groundwood Books.

Christensen, Linda. 2017. *Reading, Writing, and Rising Up: Teaching About Social Justice and the Power of the Written Word*. 2nd Edition. Milwaukee, WI: Rethinking Schools.

Cisneros, Ernesto. 2020. *Efrén Divided*. New York: Harper.

Coker, David, and William E. Lewis. 2008. "Beyond Writing Next: A Discussion of Writing Research and Instructional Uncertainty." *Harvard Educational Review* 78 (1): 231–251.

College of William & Mary. 2011. *Persuasion: Language Arts*. Dubuque, IA: Kendall Hunt.

Cooperative Children's Book Center. 2021. "CCBC Diversity Statistics." Accessed March 25, 2022. ccbc.education.wisc.edu/literature-resources/ccbc-diversity-statistics/.

Cummings, Jack A., and R. Brett Nelson. 1980. "Basic Concepts in the Oral Directions of Group Achievement Tests." *Journal of Educational Research* 73 (5): 259–261.

D'Amico, Antonella, Maurizio Cardaci, Santo Di Nuovo, and Jack Naglieri. 2012. "Differences in Achievement Not in Intelligence in the North and South of Italy: Comments on Lynn (2010a, 2010b)." *Learning and Individual Differences* 22 (1): 128–132.

Del Rizzo, Suzanne. 2017. *My Beautiful Birds*. Toronto: Pajama Press.

Dionne, Evette. 2020. *Lifting as We Climb: Black Women's Battle for the Ballot Box*. New York: Penguin Young Readers Group.

Domenech, Dan, Morton Sherman, and John Brown. 2016. *Personalizing 21st Century Education: A Framework for Student Success*. San Francisco: Jossey-Bass.

Durtschi, Melissa Dayle. 2019. "Inclusive Pathways to Gifted Education: Examining Gifted Referral Processes." Dissertation, University of Colorado at Denver.

Ecker-Lyster, Meghan, and Christopher Niileksela. 2017. "Enhancing Gifted Education for Underrepresented Students: Promising Recruitment and Programming Strategies." *Journal for the Education of the Gifted* 40 (1): 79–95.

The Education Justice Research and Organizing Collaborative. 2020. *Culturally Responsive Curriculum Scorecard Toolkit*. New York: Metropolitan Center for Research on Equity and the Transformation of Schools, New York University. steinhardt.nyu.edu/metrocenter/ejroc/culturally-responsive-curriculum-scorecard-toolkit.

Edwards, Oliver, and Thomas Oakland. 2006. "Factorial Invariance of Woodcock-Johnson III Scores for African Americans and Caucasians Americans." *Journal of Psychoeducational Assessment* 24 (4): 358–366.

Ellis, Mark. 2019. *Knowing and Valuing Every Learner: Nora's Story about Culturally Responsive Mathematics Teaching.* i-Ready Classroom Mathematics. curriculumassociates.com/-/media/fc513b83d7674cc4816f813a25076c09.ashx.

Engle, Randall, Julie Carullo, and Kathryn Collins. 1991. "Individual Differences in Working Memory for Comprehension and Following Directions." *Journal of Educational Research* 84 (5): 253–262.

Farrell, Kate. 2020. *V Is for Voting.* New York: Henry Holt and Company.

Ferlazzo, Larry. 2020. "Nine Mistakes Educators Make When Teaching English Language Learners." *Education Week*, October 26, 2020. edweek.org/teaching-learning/opinion-nine-mistakes-educators-make-when-teaching-english-language-learners/2020/10.

Ford, Donna. 2013. "Multicultural Issues: Gifted Underrepresentation and Prejudice—Learning from Allport and Merton." *Gifted Child Today* 36 (1): 62–67.

———. 2012a. "Multi-Cultural Theory and Gifted Education: Implications for the Identification of Two Underrepresented Groups." In *Identification: The Theory and Practice of Identifying Students for Gifted and Talented Education Services*, edited by Scott Hunsaker, 75–97. Mansfield Center, CT: Creative Learning Press.

———. 2012b. "Underrepresentation of Culturally Different Students in Gifted Education: Reflections About Current Problems and Recommendations for the Future." *Gifted Child Today* 33 (3): 31–35.

———. 2014a. "Multicultural Issues: Gifted Education Discrimination in 'McFadden v. Board of Education for Illinois School District U-46': A Clarion Call to School Districts, State Departments of Education, and Advocacy Organizations." *Gifted Child Today* 37 (3): 188–193.

———. 2014b. "Segregation and the Underrepresentation of Blacks and Hispanics in Gifted Education: Social Inequality and Deficit Paradigms." *Roeper Review* 36 (3): 143–154.

Ford, Donna Y., Kenneth T. Dickson, Joy Lawson Davis, Michelle Trotman Scott, and Tarek C. Grantham. 2018. "A Culturally Responsive Equity-Based Bill of Rights for Gifted Students of Color." *Gifted Child Today* 41 (3): 125–129.

Ford, Donna, J. John Harris III, Karen S. Webb, and Deneese L. Jones. 1994. "Rejection or Confirmation of Cultural Identity: A Dilemma for High-Achieving Blacks?" *Journal of Educational Thought* 28 (1): 7–33.

Gagné, Francoys. 1999. "Gagné's Differentiated Model of Giftedness and Talent (DMGT)." *Journal for the Education of the Gifted* 22 (2): 230–234.

Gentry, Marcia, Anne Gray, Gilman Whiting, Yukiko Maeda, and Nielsen Pereira. 2019. *System Failure: Access Denied: Gifted Education in the United States: Laws, Access, Equity, and Missingness Across the Country by Locale, Title I School Status, and Race.* West Lafayette, IN: Purdue University.

Gibbons, Aisa, and Russell Warne. 2019. "First Publication of Subtests in the Stanford-Binet 5, WAIS-IV, WISC-V, and WPPSI-IV." Intelligence 75 (July–August 2019): 9–18.

Gill, Cindy, Laura Moorer-Cook, Erika Armstrong, and Kristen Gill. 2012. "The Ability to Follow Verbal Directions: Identifying Skill Levels and Measuring Progress." *Canadian Journal of Speech-Language Pathology and Audiology* 36 (3): 234–247.

Graham, Steve. 2008. *Effective Writing Instruction for All Students.* Wisconsin Rapids, WI: Renaissance Learning.

Grantham, Tarek C. 2004. "Multicultural Mentoring to Increase Black Male Representation in Gifted Programs." *Gifted Child Quarterly* 48 (3): 232–245.

Gratz, Alan. 2017. *Refugee.* New York: Scholastic Press.

Hammond, Zaretta. 2015. *Culturally Responsive Teaching and the Brain: Promoting Authentic Engagement and Rigor Among Culturally and Linguistically Diverse Students.* Thousand Oaks, CA: Corwin.

Hernandez, Carlos. 2019. *Sal and Gabi Break the Universe.* New York: Disney Hyperion.

Hodges, Jaret, Jason McIntosh, and Marcia Gentry. 2017. "The Effect of an Out-of-School Enrichment Program on the Academic Achievement of High-Potential Students from Low-Income Families." *Journal of Advanced Academics* 28 (3): 204–224.

Ife, Jim. 2012. *Human Rights and Social Work: Towards Rights-Based Practice.* Cambridge: Cambridge University Press.

Johnson, Alisa. 2021. "The Culturally Responsive Teacher." Presentation at the Arizona School Administrators Conference, June 15, 2021. Tucson, AZ.

Kahn, Elizabeth. 2009. "From the Secondary Section: Making Writing Instruction Authentic." *The English Journal* 98 (5): 15–17.

Kamkwamba, William, and Bryan Mealer. 2009. *The Boy Who Harnessed the Wind: Creating Currents of Electricity and Hope.* New York: William Morrow.

Kaufman, Alan S. 2006. Foreword to the *Wechsler Nonverbal Scale of Ability Administration and Scoring Manual.* San Antonio: Pearson.

Kaufman, Alan, Susan Engi Raiford, and Diane Coalson. 2016. *Intelligent Testing with the WISC-V.* Hoboken, NJ: John Wiley & Sons.

Kaya, Fatih, Laura Stough, and Joyce Juntune. 2016. "The Effect of Poverty on the Verbal Scores of Gifted Students." *Educational Studies* 42 (1): 85–97.

Kurtz, Holly, Sterling Lloyd, Alex Harwin, Victor Chen, and Yukiko Furuya. 2019. "Gifted Education: Results of a National Survey." Bethesda, MD: Editorial Projects in Education, EdWeek Research Center.

Ladson-Billings, Gloria. 1994. *The Dreamkeepers: Successful Teachers of African American Children*. San Francisco: Jossey-Bass.

———. 1995. "Toward a Theory of Culturally Relevant Pedagogy." *American Educational Research Journal* 32 (3): 465–491.

———. 2009. "Foreword" In *Beats, Rhymes, and Classroom Life: Hip-Hop Pedagogy and the Politics of Identity*, edited by M. L. Hill, vii–x. New York: Teachers College Press.

———. 2014. "Culturally Relevant Pedagogy 2.0: A.k.a. The Remix." *Harvard Educational Review* 84 (1): 74.

Lichtenberger, Elizabeth, Marlene Sotelo-Dynega, and Alan Kaufman. 2009. "The Kaufman Assessment Battery for Children—Second Edition." In *Practitioner's Guide to Assessing Intelligence and Achievement*, edited by Jack Naglieri and Sam Goldstein, 61–94. Hoboken, NJ: John Wiley & Sons.

Lohman, David, and Elizabeth Hagen. 2001. *Cognitive Abilities Test (Form 6)*. Itasca, IL: Riverside Publishing.

Lohman, David, Katrina Korb, and Joni Lakin. 2008. "Identifying Academically Gifted English-Language Learners Using Nonverbal Tests: A Comparison of the Raven, NNAT, and CogAT." *Gifted Child Quarterly* 52 (4): 275–296.

Lynn, Richard. 2010. "In Italy, North–South Differences in IQ Predict Differences in Income, Education, Infant Mortality, Stature, and Literacy." *Intelligence* 38 (1): 93–100.

Matarazzo, Joseph. 1972. *Wechsler's Measurement and Appraisal of Adult Intelligence*. Baltimore, MD: Williams and Wilkins.

McFadden v. Board of Education for Illinois School District U-46, 984 F. Supp.2d882 (2013).

Naglieri, Jack. 1982. "Does the WISC-R Measure Verbal Intelligence for Non-English-Speaking Children?" *Psychology in the Schools* 19: 478–479.

———. 1986. "WISC-R and K-ABC Comparison for Matched Samples of Black and White Children." *Journal of School Psychology* 24: 81–88.

———. 2008. "Traditional IQ: 100 Years of Misconception and its Relationship to Minority Representation in Gifted Programs." In *Alternative Assessment of Gifted Learners (Critical Issues in Equity and Excellence in Gifted Education Series)*, edited by Joyce VanTassel-Baska, 67–88. Waco, TX: Prufrock Press.

———. 2022. *Naglieri General Ability Test-Nonverbal*. Toronto: MHS.

Naglieri, Jack, Ashley Booth, and Adam Winsler. 2004. "Comparison of Hispanic Children with and without Limited English Proficiency on the Naglieri Nonverbal Ability Test." *Psychological Assessment* 16 (1): 81–84.

Naglieri, Jack, and Dina Brulles. 2022. *Naglieri General Ability Test-Verbal.* Toronto: MHS.

Naglieri, Jack, Dina Brulles, and Kimberly Lansdowne. 2009. *Helping All Gifted Children Learn: A Teacher's Guide to Using the NNAT2.* San Antonio, TX: Pearson.

———. 2021. *Naglieri General Ability Tests Manual.* Toronto: MHS.

Naglieri, Jack, and J. P. Das. 2006. *Cognitive Assessment System—Adattamento italiano a cura di S. Taddei.* Firenze, Italy: OS.

Naglieri, Jack, J. P. Das, and Sam Goldstein. 2014a. *Cognitive Assessment System Second Edition.* Austin, TX: ProEd.

———. 2014b. *Cognitive Assessment System Second Edition: Brief.* Austin, TX: ProEd.

Naglieri, Jack, and Donna Y. 2003. "Addressing Under-representation of Gifted Minority Children Using the Naglieri Nonverbal Ability Test (NNAT)." *Gifted Child Quarterly* 47 (2): 155–160.

———. 2005. "Increasing Minority Children's Participation in Gifted Classes Using the NNAT: A Response to Lohman." *Gifted Child Quarterly* 49 (1): 29–36.

Naglieri, Jack, and Kimberly Lansdowne. 2022. *Naglieri General Ability Test-Quantitative.* Toronto: MHS.

Naglieri, Jack, and Tulio M. Otero. 2017. *Essentials of CAS2 Assessment.* New York: Wiley.

Naglieri, Jack, and Eric B. Pickering. 2010. *Helping Children Learn: Intervention Handouts for Use at School and Home (Second Edition).* Baltimore, MD: Brookes Publishing.

Naglieri, Jack, Johannes Rojahn, Holly Matto, and Sally Aquilino. 2005. "Black-White Differences in Intelligence: A Study of the Planning, Attention, Simultaneous, and Successive Theory of Intelligence." *Journal of Psychoeducational Assessment* 23 (2): 146–160.

Naglieri, Jack, and Margaret Ronning. 2000. "Comparison of White, African American, Hispanic, and Asian Children on the Naglieri Nonverbal Ability Test." *Psychological Assessment* 12 (3): 328–334.

Naglieri, Jack, and Cecelia Yazzie. 1983. "Comparison of the WISC-R and PPVT-R with Navajo Children." *Journal of Clinical Psychology* 39 (4): 598–600.

National Assessment of Educational Progress (NAEP). 2017. The Nation's Report Card. Washington, DC: U.S. Department of Education. Retrieved from nationsreportcard.gov.

National Association for Gifted Children (NAGC). NAGC Position Statements & Framing Papers. Accessed March 25, 2022. nagc.org/about-nagc/nagc-position-statements-framing-papers.

———. 2020. "Championing Equity and Supporting Social Justice for Black Students in Gifted Education: An Expanded Vision for NAGC." July 14, 2020. nagc.org/championing-equity-and-supporting-social-justice-black-students-gifted-education-expanded-vision.

Office for Civil Rights. 2016. "2013–2014 Civil Rights Data Collection: A First Look: Key Data Highlights on Equity and Opportunity Gaps in Our Nation's Public Schools." Washington, DC: US Department of Education, Office for Civil Rights.

———. 2021. "Education in a Pandemic: The Disparate Impacts of COVID-19 on America's Students." Washington, DC: US Department of Education, Office for Civil Rights.

Olszewski-Kubilius, Paula, and Jane Clarenbach. 2014. "Closing the Opportunity Gap: Program Factors Contributing to Academic Success in Culturally Different Youth." *Gifted Child Today* 37 (2): 107–110.

Ordway, Denise-Marie. 2017. "Minority Teachers: How Students Benefit from Having Teachers of Same Race." *The Journalist's Resource*, May 22, 2017. journalistsresource.org/education/minority-teachers-students-same-race-research/.

Otis, Arthur, and Roger Lennon. 2003. *Otis-Lennon School Ability Test (Eighth Edition)*. San Antonio, TX: Pearson.

Peoples, Leah Q., Tahia Islam, and Timothy Davis. 2021. *The Culturally Responsive-Sustaining STEAM Curriculum Scorecard*. New York: Metropolitan Center for Research on Equity and the Transformation of Schools, New York University. steinhardt.nyu.edu/sites/default/files/2021-02/CRSE-STEAMScorecard_FIN_optimized%20%281%29.pdf.

Peters, Scott. 2017. "Should Millions of Students Take a Gap Year? Large Numbers of Students Start the School Year Above Grade Level." *Gifted Child Quarterly* 61 (3): 229–238.

Peters, Scott, and Dina Brulles. 2017. *Designing Gifted Education Programs and Services: From Purpose to Implementation*. Waco, TX: Prufrock Press.

Peters, Scott J., and Kenneth G. Engerrand. 2016. "Equity and Excellence: Proactive Efforts in the Identification of Underrepresented Students for Gifted and Talented Services." *Gifted Child Quarterly* 60 (3): 159–171.

Peters, Scott J., Marcia Gentry, Gilman W. Whiting, and Matthew T. McBee. 2019a. "Who Gets Served in Gifted Education? Demographic Representation and a Call for Action." *Gifted Child Quarterly* 63 (4): 273–287.

———. 2020. "Reflections on the Registered Report Process for 'Effect of Local Norms on Racial and Ethnic Representation in Gifted Education.'" *AERA Open* 6 (2).

Pintner, Rudolf. 1923. *Intelligence Testing: Methods and Results*. New York: H. Holt and Company.

Plucker, Jonathan A., Scott J. Peters, and Stephanie Schmalensee. 2017. "Reducing Excellence Gaps: A Research-Based Model." *Gifted Child Today* 40 (4): 245–250.

Salkind, Neil. 2018. *Tests and Measurement for People Who (Think They) Hate Tests and Measurement*. Thousand Oaks, CA: Sage.

Selvamenan, Mathangi, Angelina Paolozza, J. Solomon, Jack A. Naglieri, and M. T. Schmidt. (2022). *Race, Ethnic, Gender, and Parental Education Level Differences on Verbal, Nonverbal, and Quantitative Naglieri General Ability Tests: Achieving Equity*. Manuscript submitted for publication.

Schrank, Fredrick A., Kevin S. McGrew, Nancy Mather, and Richard W. Woodcock. *Woodcock-Johnson IV*. Rolling Meadows, IL: Riverside Publishing.

Snyder, Thomas D., Cristobal de Brey, and Sally A. Dillow. 2019. "Digest of Education Statistics, 2017." Washington, DC: National Center for Education Statistics.

Sorell, Traci. 2018. *We Are Grateful: Otsaliheliga*. Watertown, MA: Charlesbridge.

Sotelo-Dynega, Marlene, Samuel Ortiz, Dawn Flanagan, and William Chaplin. 2013. "English Language Proficiency and Test Performance: An Evaluation of Bilingual Students with the Woodcock-Johnson III Tests of Cognitive Abilities." *Psychology in the Schools* 50 (8): 781–797.

Sullivan, Amanda. 2011. "Disproportionality in Special Education Identification and Placement of English Language Learners." *Exceptional Children* 77 (3): 317–334.

Suzuki, Lisa, and Richard Valencia. 1997. "Race–Ethnicity and Measured Intelligence: Educational Implications." *American Psychologist* 52 (10): 1103–1114.

US Department of Education. 2021. "U.S. Department of Education Fact Sheet: American Rescue Plan Act of 2021: Elementary and Secondary School Emergency Relief Fund (ARP ESSER)." oese.ed.gov/files/2021/03/FINAL_ARP-ESSER-FACT-SHEET.pdf.

Villalobos, Juan Pablo. 2019. *The Other Side: Stories of Central American Teen Refugees Who Dream of Crossing the Border*. Translated by Rosalind Harvey. New York: Farrar Straus Giroux Books for Young Readers.

Wallace, Sandra Neil, Rich Wallace, and Charly Palmer. 2020. *The Teachers March! How Selma's Teachers Changed History*. New York: Calkins Creek.

Wasserman, J. D., and K. A. Becker. 2000. "Racial and Ethnic Group Mean Score Differences on Intelligence Tests." In "Making Assessment More Fair: Taking Verbal and Achievement Out of Ability Tests." Jack A. Naglieri, chair. Symposium conducted at the annual meeting of the American Psychological Association, August 2000, Washington, DC.

Wechsler, David. 1939. *The Measurement of Adult Intelligence*. Baltimore, MD: Williams and Wilkins.

Wechsler, David, and Jack Naglieri. 2006. *Wechsler Nonverbal Scale of Ability*. San Antonio, TX: Pearson.

Wells, April. 2020. *Achieving Equity in Gifted Programming: Dismantling Barriers and Tapping Potential*. New York: Routledge.

Winebrenner, Susan, with Dina Brulles. 2018. *Teaching Gifted Kids in Today's Classroom: Strategies and Techniques Every Teacher Can Use (Updated 4th Edition)*. Minneapolis, MN: Free Spirit Publishing.

Winn, Maisha T., and Latrise Johnson. 2011. *Writing Instruction in the Culturally Relevant Classroom*. Washington, DC: National Council of Teachers of English.

Yoakum, Clarence, and Robert Yerkes. 1920. *Army Mental Tests*. New York: Henry Holt and Company.

Zalben, Jane Breskin. 2018. *A Moon for Moe and Mo*. Watertown, MA: Charlesbridge.

Index

f denotes figure

Del Rizzo, Suzanne, 113

Delisle, Jim, 51

developmental considerations, of gifted children from underrepresented populations, 94–95, 96

Digest of Education Statistics, demographic information about students, 9

Dionne, Evette, 116

disproportionality, defined, 74

district departments, collaboration with, 87–92

diversity
    defined, 1–2
    embracing of, 94–95
    glossary of terms for as related to gifted programming, 73–75

diversity, equity, and inclusion (DEI), in gifted identification and programming, 1–2

Dombrowski, Stefan C., 18

Douglass, Frederick, 116

Dunbar, Paul Laurence, 113

Durtschi, Melissa Dayle, 22

E

EdWeek, article about English language learners, 79–80

EEOA (Equal Educational Opportunities Act), 53

Efrén Divided (Cisneros), 101

Ellis, Mark, 114

engineering, as way to expand perspective, 115

Engle, Randall, 23

English language learner (ELL) students
    characteristics of gifted ones, 84–85
    disparities in outcomes for, 1
    disproportionate numbers of in gifted education programs, 3, 8, 9, 28, 77
    enrolled in US public schools, 11–12*f*
    language support for gifted ones, 84
    obstacles and solutions for, 79–80
    testing accommodations for, 36
    and universal testing, 55

environmental considerations, of gifted children from underrepresented populations, 95, 96–97

Equal Educational Opportunities Act (EEOA), 54

equity
    achieving of in gifted programming, 72–98
    considerations for in gifted programming models, 86–87*f*
    defined, 2, 74, 80
    differentiating between test bias and, 13

in gifted education, call for, 1

and test scores and identifying gifted students, 20–22

equity specialists, role of in building equity in gifted programming, 91

Equity-Based Bill of Rights for Gifted Students of Color, 77, 78

ethnicity, intelligence test mean standard score differences by, 20–21*f*

F

Farrell, Kate, 115

Ferlazzo, Larry, 79–80

504 Accommodation Plans, testing accommodations for students with, 36

Flesch-Kincaid Grade Level method, 22

flexible grouping
    as gifted programming model, 87*f*
    use of, 81–84

Ford, Donna, 9, 21, 22, 77, 80, 87

G

Galbraith, Judy, 51

Gandhi, Mahatma, 116

general ability
    high general ability without high achievement, 78–79
    measurement of, 18, 24
    use of term, 17

Gentry, Marcia, 10

gifted, use of term, 2

gifted education/programming
    achieving equity in, 72–98
    approaches for serving underrepresented populations, 80–98
    considerations for equity in models of, 86–87*f*
    elephant in the room regarding, 8–16
    glossary of terms for diversity as related to, 73–75
    inequities in, 9, 10*f*, 11, 76, 79
    redesigning policies of, 77
    redesigns of, 75–76
    use of local or building norms in, 85

gifted identification
    ability tests for, 17–29
    challenges in, 8–9
    equity and test scores and, 20–22
    next steps after, 68–69
    screening versus, 52–53
    tips for success in testing of, 34

gifted population, understanding yours, 96–98

The Gifted Teen Survival Guide (Galbraith and Delisle), 51

giftedness
    levels of, 49*f*

percent of schools in US not assessing for, 10

Gigena, Florencia, 113

Gill, Cindy, 23

Google Classroom, 38

Google Meet, 38

Gorman, Amanda, 116

Graham, Steve, 116

grants coordinator, role of in building equity in gifted programming, 90

Gratz, Alan, 113

grouping, use of cluster grouping and flexible grouping, 81–84, 87*f*

H

Harkness Circle, 114

Hernandez, Carlos, 113

Hispanic students
    accurate assessment of, 15
    disparities in outcomes for, 1
    disproportionate numbers of in gifted education programs, 3, 8, 9, 28, 76–77
    effectiveness of NNAT in identifying gifted students, 21
    number of English language learner (ELL) Hispanic students enrolled in US public schools, 12*f*
    number of enrolled in US public schools in 2018, 10*f*
    and relationship between race and identification rates, 22
    and universal testing, 54–55

honors classes, as gifted programming model, 86*f*

Hughes, Langston, 113

human resources, role of in building equity in gifted programming, 88–89

I

identity group considerations, of gifted children from underrepresented populations, 95–96, 97–98

inclusion, defined, 2, 74

inclusionary services, defined, 74

Individualized Education Programs (IEP), testing accommodations for students with, 36

instructional approaches
    culturally responsive approaches. *See* culturally responsive approaches/practices
    examination of, 105–106
    for serving underrepresented populations of gifted students, 80–98
    strengths-based approach, 79, 85, 107
    systems approach, 87

intelligence

About the Authors

Dina Brulles, Ph.D., is the gifted program coordinator at Arizona State University and the former gifted education director at Paradise Valley Unified School District. She serves as governance secretary on the NAGC Board of Directors, and previously as NAGC's school district representative. Dina's work and publications center on increasing inclusion and building equity in gifted education programs and services using culturally responsive practices. Dina has authored numerous articles and chapters and coauthored books, including *A Teacher's Guide to Flexible Grouping and Collaborative Learning*; *Designing Gifted Education Programs*; *The Cluster Grouping Handbook*; *Teaching Gifted Kids in Today's Classrooms*; and *Helping All Gifted Children Learn*.

Kimberly Lansdowne, Ph.D., is the founding executive director of the Herberger Young Scholars Academy, a secondary school for highly gifted students at Arizona State University (ASU). She received her doctorate at ASU and has a lengthy career in teaching and administration at universities, colleges, public and private schools. At ASU, she develops and teaches undergraduate and graduate level education classes on curriculum, instruction, testing, measurement, and special needs. Previously, Kim was the director of gifted services at Scottsdale Unified School District, a gifted specialist, a middle school math teacher, and an elementary general education teacher. She lives in Phoenix, Arizona.

Jack A. Naglieri, Ph.D., has held faculty appointments at Northern Arizona University, The Ohio State University, and George Mason University. He is currently a research professor at the University of Virginia, senior research scientist at the Devereux Center for Resilient Children, and emeritus professor of psychology at George Mason University. Dr. Naglieri has developed many tests used by psychologists and educators such as the Naglieri Nonverbal Ability Test, the Cognitive Assessment System, Autism Spectrum Rating Scale, Devereux Student Strength Assessment, and Comprehensive Executive Function Inventory. He is widely known for his efforts to increase participation of traditionally underrepresented students in gifted education and remains an active presenter on related topics. Dr. Naglieri is committed to equitable and valid assessment though high-quality tests and rating scales and a continual effort to help professionals make positive differences in the lives of the students they evaluate. He lives near Washington, D.C.

Other Great Resources from Free Spirit

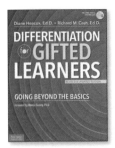

Differentiation for Gifted Learners
Going Beyond the Basics (Revised & Updated Edition)
by Diane Heacox, Ed.D., and Richard M. Cash, Ed.D.

For K–8 teachers, gifted education teachers, program directors, administrators, instructional coaches, and curriculum developers. 264 pp.; PB; 8½" x 11"; includes digital content.

Free PLC/Book Study Guide
freespirit.com/PLC

Start Seeing and Serving Underserved Gifted Students
50 Strategies for Equity and Excellence
by Jennifer Ritchotte, Ph.D., Chin-Wen Lee, Ph.D., and Amy Graefe, Ph.D.

For educators and administrators of grades K–8. 192 pp.; PB; 8½" x 11"; includes digital content.

Free PLC/Book Study Guide
freespirit.com/PLC

Teaching Gifted Kids in Today's Classroom
Strategies and Techniques Every Teacher Can Use (Updated 4th Edition)
by Susan Winebrenner, M.S., with Dina Brulles, Ph.D.

For teachers and administrators, grades K–12. 256 pp.; PB; 8½" x 11"; includes digital content.

When Gifted Kids Don't Have All the Answers
How to Meet Their Social and Emotional Needs (Revised & Updated Edition)
by Judy Galbraith, M.A., and Jim Delisle, Ph.D.

For teachers, gifted coordinators, guidance counselors, and parents of gifted children grades K–9. 288 pp.; PB; B&W photos; 7¼" x 9¼"; includes digital content.

Empowering Underrepresented Gifted Students
Perspectives from the Field
edited by Joy Lawson Davis, Ed.D., and Deb Douglas, M.S.
Grades K–12. 208 pp.; PB; 8½" x 11".

The Power of Self-Advocacy for Gifted Learners
Teaching the 4 Essential Steps to Success
by Deb Douglas

For teachers of gifted students in grades 5–12, counselors, gifted program coordinators, administrators, parents, and youth leaders. 208 pp.; PB; 8½" x 11"; includes digital content.

Free PLC/Book Study Guide
freespirit.com/PLC

Teaching Gifted Children in Today's Preschool and Primary Classrooms
Identifying, Nurturing, and Challenging Children Ages 4–9
by Joan Franklin Smutny, M.A., Sally Yahnke Walker, Ph.D., and Ellen I. Honeck, Ph.D.

For teachers of preschool, preK, K–3. 248 pp.; PB; 8½" x 11"; includes digital content.

Free PLC/Book Study Guide
freespirit.com/PLC

Bright, Complex Kids
Supporting Their Social and Emotional Development
by Jean Sunde Peterson, Ph.D., and Daniel B. Peters, Ph.D.

Grades K–12. 152 pp.; PB; 7¼" x 9¼".

Free PLC/Book Study Guide
freespirit.com/PLC

Interested in purchasing multiple quantities and receiving volume discounts?
Contact edsales@freespirit.com or call 1.800.735.7323 and ask for Education Sales.

Many Free Spirit authors are available for speaking engagements, workshops, and keynotes.
Contact speakers@freespirit.com or call 1.800.735.7323.

For pricing information, to place an order, or to request a free catalog, contact:
Free Spirit Publishing • 6325 Sandburg Road, Suite 100 • Minneapolis, MN 55427-3674
toll-free 800.735.7323 • local 612.338.2068 • fax 612.337.5050
help4kids@freespirit.com • freespirit.com